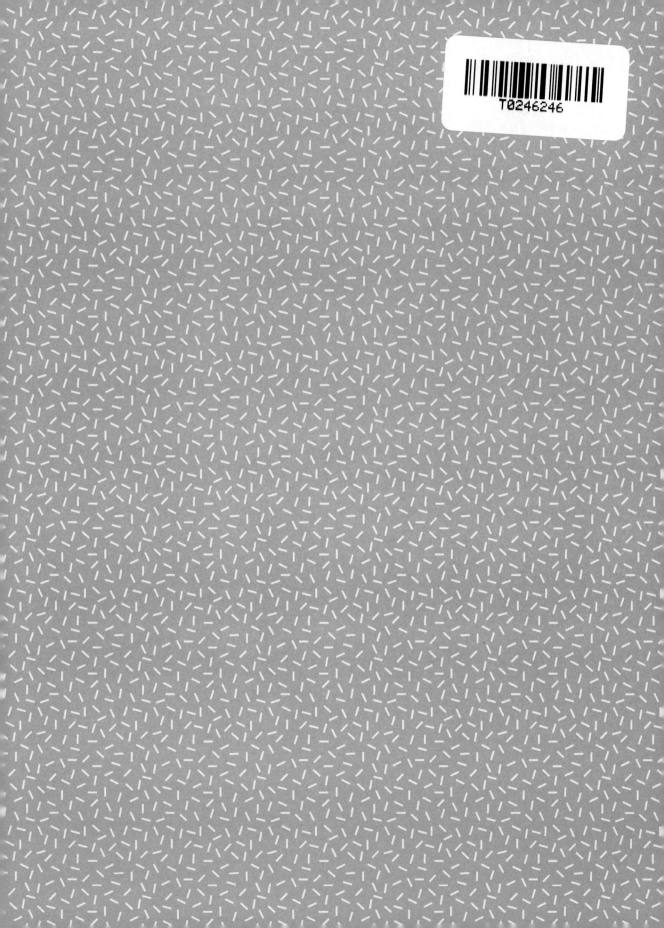

Slimming
AND
Speedy

Slimming AND Speedy

100+ Quick, Easy and Tasty Meals Under 600 Calories

LATOYAH EGERTON

CREATOR OF THE SUGAR PINK FOOD BLOG

greenfinch

CONTENTS

a little bit about this book

If you're reading this, then you're on the way to finding the secret to making mouth-watering food in as little time as possible.

My name is Latoyah and I am the creator of Sugar Pink Food, a recipe blog and online community, where I share healthy, delicious, lower-calorie meals that the whole family can enjoy, without sacrificing any flavour.

I have always had a passion for food and cooking. I grew up watching my favourite TV chefs, and when I moved out of my parents' house in my late teens I found cooking to be a great way to relax. I also loved the buzz of creating something that other people would taste and enjoy.

I initially started my blog as a place to share recipes with friends, but it gradually developed into a way of creating calorie-controlled recipes as I started on my slimming journey. Over time, it grew to be a great success with hundreds of thousands of followers and millions of views. I never expected it to grow into a career in the way that it has. This all culminated in the publication of my first book, *Slimming and Tasty*, in 2022.

Since then, I have thought more and more about how difficult it can be to find the balance between cooking homemade healthy meals and enjoying what little free time you have. I have always enjoyed cooking, but even so, there are some days when spending a long time in the kitchen preparing a meal is the last thing that I want to do. This is often when the urge to order in food, which may not be as healthy, can take over.

Slimming and Speedy is my solution. It is aimed at those of us who lead a busy life, but still want to enjoy delicious and nutritious meals with as little effort as possible.

I have always felt that creating 'weeknight recipes' is important, and they have been hugely popular with my followers. The concept is simple: meals that you can prepare or cook in as little time as possible, making them perfect for weeknight cooking when time is limited.

Slimming and Speedy aims to provide time-saving tricks and tips, using a combination of batch cooking for the week, stocking up the freezer, or meals that only take a few minutes of preparation before you can chuck them in the slow cooker to cook away while you're at work. It also includes dinners that you can whip up in as little as 15 minutes, meaning you have more time to enjoy your evenings. There are even some tasty snacks to help keep you going throughout the day, and delicious desserts for those with a sweet tooth, which are still lower in calories.

The meals are all under 600 calories, and what they lack in time to prepare, they make up for in flavour. I am proud to say that while my recipes are lower in calories, you would never believe that they are 'diet food'. I used to hate having to prepare different dishes for different people in the house, but I strongly believe that my recipes can be enjoyed by everyone, even the fussiest of foodies.

I hope that you enjoy making and tasting these recipes as much as I have enjoyed creating them, and that you discover some new family favourites that can be enjoyed time and time again!

top tips for creating speedy slimming recipes

Cooking low-calorie meals doesn't need to mean cutting out the things you love to eat. In fact, doing this can often make it harder to stick to a diet or meal plan. I think that life is too short to deny yourself a little pleasure, so instead I follow a few easy rules when creating my recipes, which you can use too.

Use lean meat
One easy, healthy choice you can make is to use lean meats when cooking, such as skinless, boneless chicken breast or lean beef or lean turkey mince that is 5% fat or less. For any meats that are naturally fattier, you can trim off any excess.

For some fatty cuts of meat like bacon, search out alternatives like bacon medallions instead of trimming off the excess, as this also saves on waste.

Swap in low-fat cheese and dairy
A simple swap you can make is to change your cheese to a low-fat alternative and use low-fat cream cheese as a replacement for cream. Low-fat cream cheese helps to make deliciously creamy sauces without as much fat as using butter and cream.

Use as little sugar as possible
I try to use as little sugar as possible in my cooking. Of course, some foods such as fruit naturally contain sugars, but I try to avoid adding any extra sugar to my recipes. A simple swap from sugar to sweetener is easy when making things like BBQ sauce.

Swap oil for low-fat cooking spray
Another great way to save on calories is to replace butter or oil in your frying pan with low-calorie cooking spray.

Eat smaller portions

I find it is better to have smaller portion sizes of a core dish, which you can then bulk out with extra vegetables. For years I ate absolutely huge plates of food, thinking that I was being good because it was slightly lower in fat. The bigger the portion, the more calories you take in.

Drink two litres of water every day

One of the most important things – which I cannot stress enough – is how drinking water helps you lose weight. When your body starts burning fat, you need to flush the fat out, and the easiest way to do so is to make sure you're drinking enough water. At first it will seem hard to do, but the more you make sure you're drinking enough, the better you will feel. Your body will also get used to it, after the first few days, and you will naturally feel thirstier

time-saving tricks

The key to many of the recipes in this book is how quickly they can be prepared, but there are also a few simple tricks that can make your life even easier – and save you even more time – when preparing weeknight meals.

Read the recipe in full before you start

While I literally write recipes for a living now, I used to struggle when following them. That's because I wouldn't read the recipe properly in full before I started. I would skim the ingredients and the method quickly, then just get going. The key to speedy recipes is knowing exactly what you have to do before you do it. Stopping to check the recipe or find which step you're on only wastes time. So read it all fully before you start, and it will make it much easier, and – more importantly – quicker, to follow.

Planning and preparation

Got a busy week ahead? Then spend some time at the weekend planning your meals. This might mean planning when to get your pre-prepared freezer bag meals out of the freezer to defrost overnight, batch cooking so you have meals ready to reheat in the evenings, or making some overnight oats to be enjoyed for breakfast.

Organise your tools

Get everything that the recipe requires out and ready to go before you get started, such as pans, knives, seasonings and ingredients. You'll be cooking like you're on a TV food show in no time!

Multi-tasking

If you are making a meal that requires pasta, for example, then get this cooking and on the go while you prepare the rest of the meal. This may seem obvious, but it saves so much time.

Use frozen pre-sliced vegetables

You can now buy frozen pre-sliced vegetables, such as peppers and onions, from most supermarkets, which can save you a lot of prep time. It's also just as easy to slice and freeze vegetables yourself if you don't want to buy them ready-made: it only takes a few minutes to do, and can really help you when making your meals. The best way to freeze them yourself is to slice them all up, then spread the slices out in a single layer of a baking tray, so that the slices aren't touching. Freeze them until solid, then transfer them to a freezer bag to store in the freezer.

Try 'lazy garlic' and 'lazy ginger'
A few of these recipes require ginger or garlic, and for convenience I really recommend using the 'lazy' jars, which are pre-diced garlic and ginger, so you just add them by the teaspoon.

Go for microwave rice
I am a huge fan of microwave rice. It is obviously much quicker to prepare and is great when adding it directly into a meal too. I just use the plain versions, and you can also get some good boil-in-the-bag rice which is still quick to prepare as well.

Clean as you go
Another tip which may seem obvious, but cleaning as you go saves time overall and also helps to make the cooking process more streamlined. A tidy workspace makes cooking much easier and helps with space – a tidy space makes my mind feel tidier too.

Put the lid on
When cooking pasta, vegetables or simmering sauces, put the lid on the saucepan. This helps to cook things quicker by keeping the heat in.

Chop veg into smaller chunks
The smaller you chop up your veggies, the less time it takes to cook them through, especially with things like potatoes.

before you get started

While I have calculated calories to the best of my ability, there is always room for variables based on the particular brands that you may use, or small variations in weight. I always recommend double-checking the calories if you deviate from the recipe or are following a strict calorie plan.

Ovens and hobs vary, even if cooking at the same temperature. Make sure to preheat your oven before cooking and always check food is fully cooked before eating, especially for fish, seafood, and meats like chicken. The best way to check if the chicken is cooked is to make sure it is no longer pink in the middle. If using a meat thermometer, chicken should register 75°C to 80°C (167°F to 176°F) in the thickest part.

Chicken breast weights and sizes can vary, but I work on the general rule of one breast per person. When chicken is used, make sure it is always skinless as this makes it as lean as possible.

There are loads of low-calorie cooking sprays on the market, and you can use any based on your preference. The majority are zero calories per spray. You can also get olive oil sprays, which allow you to use real oil, but much less of it. Double-check the calories on these and adjust when required.

Icons
The following icons are used in the book:

⊘ Vegetarian

Ⓥ Vegan

⊛ Gluten-free

⊜ Dairy-free

A lot of my recipes are easily adaptable to suit a vegetarian or vegan diet, and I have included notes and suggested swaps where applicable. You may need to adjust the calorie count based on what ingredients you use.

Slow cookers

Any slow cooker recipes have been based on a standard-sized 3.5-litre slow cooker. If you don't have a slow cooker, I would really recommend getting one. You can pick them up for as little as £20 nowadays, and they help save time and produce so many delicious meals.

Air fryers

Most air fryer recipes can also be cooked in the oven, and there are notes in each recipe to advise how to.

Freezer bags

When using freezer bags, ensure that you squeeze all air out as much as possible, flatten out and seal. Make sure that you date and label the freezer bags with the contents and the date it was prepared so that you don't lose track. I use the XL bags, which are Gallon Freezer Bags or 3.79 litres.

Freezer trays

A lot of dishes can be frozen in a tray that can also be put straight into the oven. I use foil trays for any pasta dishes I intend to freeze. You can pick these up very cheaply at £1 shops.

Freezing and defrosting

For the freezer meals, each recipe has individual instructions on how to store it. It is really important to make sure that the food is fully cooked or reheated before serving. Most dishes require you to defrost them overnight in the refrigerator before cooking.

BREAKFASTS

IN A HURRY

Have you ever noticed when you eat
breakfast in the morning that you're always
much hungrier by lunchtime than when you
don't? Breakfast is such an important meal,
and eating a balanced breakfast can help
kickstart your metabolism.

Breakfast can be so much more than boring
cereal or toast, there are just so many
delicious and simple breakfasts that you
can create. The possibilities are endless!

When we are busy getting ready to get
out of the door for work in the mornings,
breakfast can often fall by the wayside,
as we opt to grab something on the way to
work, or swap a meal for a massive coffee.
I love eating a cooked, warm breakfast in
the mornings, however, even when I am busy
on the weekend.

This chapter includes a selection of
breakfasts that are quick to prepare in the
mornings or can be prepared ahead of time
and left in the refrigerator overnight so
that you can eat them first thing, including
some of my favourite overnight oat recipes.

Breakfast doesn't have to be as time-
consuming as you may think…

banana bread pancakes

I swear that when I buy bananas, I almost never eat them before they start to go brown. This means I often end up making them into banana bread, which isn't as healthy as I had originally intended them to be. This recipe has all those delicious banana bread flavours in breakfast form, and is much better for you!

**MAKES 1 PORTION
(4 PANCAKES PER PORTION)**

2 medium eggs

40g (1½oz) porridge oats

1 ripe banana, peeled and mashed

2 tablespoons fat-free Greek yoghurt

1 tablespoon granulated sweetener

½ teaspoon vanilla extract

½ teaspoon ground cinnamon

Low-calorie cooking spray

To serve

½ banana, sliced

1 tablespoon maple syrup

Prep time 5 minutes | **Cook time** 10 minutes | **Calorie count** 548 calories per portion

Separate the egg whites from the yolks, putting them in separate, clean bowls.

Whisk the egg whites in a clean bowl with a hand-held electric whisk until they are light and fluffy and have formed stiff peaks.

Blitz the oats in a food processor or blender until finely ground.

Mix the egg yolks, mashed banana, yoghurt, sweetener, vanilla extract and cinnamon, then gently fold in the egg whites and stir to form the pancake batter.

Heat a frying pan (skillet) over a medium heat, spray with some low-calorie cooking spray and add a dollop of pancake mixture to the middle of the pan. Cook for 2 minutes, then use a spatula to flip the pancake over. Repeat until the mixture is used up (the mixture should give you 4 pancakes).

Serve with the sliced banana and maple syrup.

Note The trick to making these pancakes extra fluffy is to whisk the egg whites to the perfect peaks.

mixed berry french toast cups

French toast is something that I really enjoy having as a treat, and these French toast cups are little bites of heaven. They are matched perfectly with the mixed berries and maple syrup. They can also be cooked in an air fryer if you have silicone muffin cups.

MAKES 4 PORTIONS

4 large eggs
150ml (5fl oz/¾ cup) skimmed milk (or non-dairy alternative)
1 teaspoon vanilla extract
1 teaspoon ground cinnamon
1 teaspoon granulated sweetener
4 slices of wholemeal bread
4 strawberries, hulled and sliced
8 raspberries
20 blueberries
Low-calorie cooking spray

To serve
4 tablespoons fat-free Greek yoghurt
4 tablespoons maple syrup

Prep time 5 minutes | **Cook time** 10 minutes | **Calorie count** 480 calories per portion

Preheat the oven 200°C/180°C fan/400°F/Gas mark 6 and spray 4 holes of a muffin tin with low-calorie cooking spray.

Whisk the eggs with the milk, vanilla extract, cinnamon and sweetener in a shallow bowl until well combined.

Use a rolling pin to roll out the bread slices so that they are thinner and larger. Dip the bread into the egg mixture and allow it to soak up the mixture for a few seconds, then remove the bread. Allow any excess mixture to drip off, then press the bread slice down into the muffin tin holes to form cups. Bake in the oven for 10 minutes, keeping an eye on them to make sure they don't burn.

Fill each baked cup with the berries while it's still warm, spoon on the yoghurt and drizzle with maple syrup.

~~~~~

Notes Rolling out the bread makes it thinner and helps it to cook quicker in the oven, as well as making a bigger cup.

The cups can be refrigerated for up to 3 days in a sealed container.

chocolate and caramel cheesecake overnight oats

The idea is simple: prepare this dish overnight and it is ready for when you need it in the morning. This is for anyone who has a sweet tooth – it tastes just like a Mars bar!

**MAKES 1 LARGE OR
2 SMALLER PORTIONS**

40g (1½oz) porridge oats

1½ tablespoons skimmed milk
    or almond milk

3 tablespoons vanilla
    protein yoghurt (or fat-
    free Greek yoghurt)

1 tablespoon biscuit spread
    (such as Biscoff)

30g (1oz) milk chocolate

2 teaspoons fat-free Greek
    yoghurt

Your choice of fresh fruit,
    to serve

Prep time 5 minutes, plus overnight chilling time |
Calorie count 435 calories per large portion

Put the oats in a small dish that you can cover overnight, or a Tupperware container with a lid. Add the milk, mix and press down to form the base. Add the protein yoghurt and smooth it down with a spatula.

Melt the biscuit spread in a microwaveable bowl in the microwave in short 10-second bursts, then pour this over the top of the protein yoghurt.

Melt the chocolate in a microwaveable bowl in the microwave in short 10-second bursts and mix it with the Greek yoghurt to form a ganache, then pour over the top. Smooth over the surface and refrigerate overnight. Serve the next day with fresh fruit.

Note This makes 1 large portion, but can be split to make 2 smaller portions for half the calories.

peanut butter brownie overnight oats

One for the peanut butter fans...Chocolate and peanut butter just seem to go together so well, and this overnight oats recipe will certainly not disappoint! Serve with your choice of fresh fruit – I love this with banana.

**MAKES 1 LARGE OR
2 SMALLER PORTIONS**

40g (1½oz) porridge oats

2 teaspoons unsweetened cocoa powder

2 tablespoons skimmed milk

3 tablespoons vanilla protein yoghurt (or fat-free vanilla Greek yoghurt)

1 tablespoon smooth peanut butter

Your choice of fresh fruit, to serve

Prep time 5 minutes, plus overnight chilling time | **Calorie count** 520 calories per large portion

Place the oats in a small dish that you can cover overnight, or a Tupperware container with a lid. Add 1 teaspoon of the cocoa powder and all the skimmed milk, then mix well.

Add the other teaspoon of cocoa powder to the yoghurt and mix well. Add this on top of the oats and smooth over.

Melt the peanut butter in a microwaveable bowl in the microwave for 10 seconds. Pour this over the top and lift the dish/tub and move it around to help the peanut butter spread evenly over the surface.

Refrigerate overnight. Serve the next day with fresh fruit.

Note This makes 1 large portion, but can be split to make 2 smaller portions for half the calories.

chocolate and coconut overnight wheat

A fabulous overnight Weetbix recipe that reminds me of a Bounty bar. It's packed with protein too, which helps keep you feeling full all morning until lunchtime.

**MAKES 1 LARGE OR
2 SMALLER PORTIONS**

1 wheat biscuit
   (such as Weetabix)
3 tablespoons coconut
   protein yoghurt (or fat-
   free Greek yoghurt and 1
   teaspoon desiccated/dried
   shredded coconut)
2 tablespoons chocolate oat
   milk (or skimmed milk)
30g (1oz) dark chocolate
Your choice of fresh fruit,
   to serve (I love this
   with raspberries)

Prep time 5 minutes, plus overnight chilling time |
Calorie count 520 calories per large portion

Crumble the wheat biscuit into a small dish that you can cover overnight, or a Tupperware container with a lid. Add the coconut protein yoghurt and chocolate oat milk and mix well, then press down to even out the surface.

Melt the dark chocolate in a microwaveable bowl in the microwave in short 10-second bursts, then pour it over the top. Lift the dish/container and move it around to help the chocolate spread evenly.

Refrigerate overnight. Serve the next day with fresh fruit.

~~~

Note This makes 1 large portion,
but can be split to make 2 smaller
portions for half the calories.

turkish egg toasts

This is my take on a Nigella dish that I love, which itself is an interpretation of the Turkish dish *çilbir*. The original dish is a delicious dippy bowl, but I often find it too messy to eat, which is why I prefer these toasts as they can be eaten with a knife and fork. I also recommend using sourdough as it just hits differently!

MAKES 2 PORTIONS

100g (3½oz) fat-free Greek
    yoghurt
2 large garlic cloves,
    finely diced
2 large eggs
2 tablespoons low-fat butter
    spread
1 teaspoon smoked paprika
½ teaspoon dried chilli
    flakes

To serve
2 slices of sourdough
A few parsley leaves,
    chopped

Prep time 5 minutes | **Cook time** 10 minutes|
Calorie count 490 calories per portion

Combine the yoghurt and garlic in a bowl and set aside.

Poach the eggs by adding them to a saucepan of boiling water with a pinch of salt. (If you don't have really fresh eggs, add a tablespoon of white wine vinegar to the water as well, to help them hold together.) Poach for 4 minutes, then remove the eggs with a slotted spoon.

Put the butter spread in a frying pan (skillet) over a low heat. When melted, add the smoked paprika and chilli flakes and cook for a few minutes, being careful not to let the butter or spices burn.

Toast the sourdough, then cover each slice with a thick layer of the garlicky yoghurt mixture. Top with a poached egg, then drizzle with the melted chilli butter, and top with the parsley.

Notes The key to perfectly poached eggs is to use really fresh eggs.

I have used sourdough for this recipe, but use wholemeal bread if you prefer.

To make the dish gluten free, use gluten-free bread.

creamy garlic mushroom and sweet potato toast

This is a great lower-carb alternative to mushrooms on toast, and using quark means it is lower fat too. I love the creamy garlicky flavour of the mushrooms, and the sweet potato balances out the creaminess perfectly.

**MAKES 2 PORTIONS
(2 SWEET POTATO TOASTS
PER PORTION)**

1 large sweet potato
1 garlic clove, finely diced
225g (8oz) button mushrooms,
   sliced or whole
1 tablespoon quark
1 teaspoon dried parsley
Low-calorie cooking spray
Sea salt and freshly ground
   black pepper
A few parsley leaves,
   to serve

Prep time 5 minutes | **Cook time** 10 minutes |
Calorie count 200 calories per portion

Cut the sweet potato lengthways, then into slices approximately 5mm (½ inch) thick. Spray both sides of each slice with low-calorie cooking spray. Add the slices straight into your toaster and toast for 5 minutes, then check to make sure they aren't burnt and cook for a further 5 minutes.

Meanwhile, spray a saucepan with some low-calorie cooking spray and place over a medium heat. Add the garlic and fry for 2 minutes, then add the mushrooms, season with salt and pepper and cook for about 3 minutes. Stir through the quark and dried parsley.

Once the sweet potato toasts are cooked, lay them on a serving plate and spoon over the creamy garlic mushrooms. Finish with a sprinkle of parsley.

~~~

Note You can cook the sweet potato toasts directly in your toaster, or cook them under a hot grill. The thinner you slice them, the quicker they will take to cook

'posh' egg on toast

What could be so posh about egg on toast? Well, this is my spicy fried eggs with garlicky butter on wholemeal toast. Honestly, it takes the flavours to the next level! This dish is inspired by the time I stayed in a fancy hotel, and the toast was all served with garlic butter. The scrambled eggs are made in the traditional French way too, for a little extra *je ne sais quoi*.

MAKES 2 PORTIONS

2 tablespoons low-fat butter spread

1 garlic clove, finely diced

1 parsley sprig, finely chopped

3 medium eggs

½ fresh red or green chilli, deseeded and finely chopped

Low-calorie cooking spray

Sea salt and freshly ground black pepper

4 slices of wholemeal bread, to serve

Prep time 5 minutes | **Cook time** 10 minutes | **Calorie count** 420 calories per portion

To make the garlic butter, mix together the butter spread, diced garlic and chopped parsley in a bowl. Set aside while you prepare the eggs.

Crack the eggs into a jug and whisk until combined.

Spray a small saucepan with some low-calorie cooking spray and place over a medium heat. Add the fresh chilli and fry for 2 minutes, then add the whisked eggs, stirring constantly. Remove from the heat every now and again as the eggs cook, continuing to stir – this helps the egg mixture to set when removed from the heat. Continue until the egg is cooked all the way through. It is best when still slightly runny, as it continues to cook once removed from the heat.

Toast the wholemeal bread slices, then spread them with the garlic butter. Add the chilli scrambled eggs on top of the toast, and sprinkle with some salt and pepper to serve.

Note This is best served straight away, but leftover butter can be stored in the refrigerator for up to 5 days.

sticky honey, lime, halloumi and avocado wrap

Halloumi – or, as I like to call it, 'squeaky cheese' – is so delicious! Its versatility is amazing, and it's great for breakfasts. Adding lime juice and honey absolutely takes it to the next level. This tasty, simple veggie breakfast recipe has all the ingredients to become a new favourite.

MAKES 1 PORTION
For the halloumi
1 tablespoon runny honey
Juice of 1 lime
45g (1½oz) reduced-fat
   halloumi cheese, cut
   into 1.5cm (½ inch)-thick
   slices
Low-calorie cooking spray

To serve (for 1 portion)
¼ ripe avocado, peeled
5 cherry tomatoes, chopped
1 tablespoon fat-free Greek
   yoghurt
1 wholemeal flour tortilla
   wrap
Sea salt and freshly ground
   black pepper

Prep time 5 minutes | **Prep time** 10 minutes |
Calorie count 550 calories per portion/wrap

In a small bowl, mix together the lime juice and honey. Add the sliced halloumi and mix well until each slice is covered in the honey and lime mixture.

Heat a frying pan (skillet) over a medium heat and spray with some low-calorie cooking spray. Add the slices of halloumi and cook for 3 minutes on each side until golden.

Drizzle any excess honey and lime juice mixture into the pan with the halloumi and reduce the heat to allow it to thicken slightly and become sticky.

Put the avocado and chopped tomatoes into a bowl and smash them together using the back of a fork. Season with a pinch each of salt and pepper.

When ready to serve, spread the yoghurt over the tortilla wrap, then add the avocado and tomato mixture. Add the sticky halloumi slices, then fold over each side of the wrap.

Notes Make sure the pan doesn't get too hot or the halloumi could stick!

To make this gluten free, use a gluten-free wrap.

smoky spinach eggs

This is a simple yet extremely delicious dish. I love throwing this together in the morning and eating it on its own. It's low in carbs too, but you could serve it with some bread or toast if you like (just remember to adjust the calories). The smoky paprika goes perfectly with the spinach to make this dish extra enjoyable!

MAKES 2 PORTIONS

1 onion, finely diced
2 teaspoons smoked paprika
1 x 400g (14oz) tin of
  chopped tomatoes
450g (1lb) spinach leaves
Large pinch each of sea salt
  and black pepper
4 large eggs
Low-calorie cooking spray

Prep time 5 minutes | **Cook time** 10 minutes |
Calorie count 260 calories per portion

Spray a large frying pan (skillet) with some low-calorie cooking spray and place over a medium heat. Add the onion and fry for 2 minutes until softened, then add half of the smoked paprika and mix well. Add the chopped tomatoes to the pan, reduce the heat and simmer for 2 minutes.

Add the rest of the smoked paprika to the pan with the spinach, and the salt and pepper. Allow the spinach to wilt for 2 minutes, then make 4 holes in the mixture for the eggs.

Crack an egg into each hole, then add the lid to the pan (or cover it with a plate) and cook for 5 minutes (7 minutes if you don't want to have a runny yolk). Once the egg has cooked to your liking, season and serve immediately.

Note Using a frying pan (skillet) with a lid helps to steam the eggs and cook them on top.

vegan breakfast skillet

This delicious vegan recipe is perfect for meat-free days. It's packed full of flavour, and also works great as a meal prep. It's low carb too, yet super filling. Even better, it can all be cooked in one frying pan (skillet), which saves on washing up!

MAKES 2 PORTIONS

1 onion, finely diced

1 small courgette
  (zucchini), chopped

1 red (bell) pepper,
  deseeded and chopped

100g (3½oz) baby button
  mushrooms

100g (3½oz) cherry tomatoes,
  sliced

200g (7oz) baby spinach
  leaves

1 x 400g (14oz) tin of black
  beans, drained

1 x 400g (14oz) tin of
  butter beans, drained

½ teaspoon garlic granules

½ teaspoon onion powder

½ teaspoon paprika

Pinch of dried chilli (hot
  red pepper) flakes

Low-calorie cooking spray

Sea salt and freshly ground
  black pepper

Drizzle of sriracha sauce,
  to serve

Prep time 5 minutes | **Cook time** 15 minutes | **Calorie count** 350 calories per portion

Spray a large frying pan (skillet) with some low-calorie cooking spray and place over a medium heat. Add the onion, courgette, chopped pepper, mushrooms and tomatoes and cook for about 5 minutes.

Add the spinach, black beans and butter beans, then season with the garlic granules, onion powder, paprika, chilli flakes and a pinch each of salt and pepper. Reduce the heat and cook for 10 minutes until the beans have softened.

Serve immediately with a drizzle of sriracha sauce, or leave to cool before portioning up and refrigerating.

Note Cook ahead of time, portion and refrigerate for up to 5 days if you like, then reheat when you're ready to eat.

sausage and hash brown one-pan scramble

Sausages and hash browns are two absolute staples of a classic English breakfast. This amazing one-pan recipe combines all those delicious breakfast flavours, and is very filling as well, meaning there's less chance of snacking between breakfast and lunch!

MAKES 2 PORTIONS

1 onion, finely diced
1 garlic clove, finely diced
1 large potato, peeled and
    grated
Pinch each of sea salt and
    freshly ground black
    pepper
½ teaspoon smoked paprika
250g (9oz) extra-lean 5%-fat
    minced (ground) pork
1 teaspoon dried sage
10 cherry tomatoes, halved
Handful of spinach leaves
2 large eggs
Low-calorie cooking spray
40g (1½oz) reduced-fat feta
    cheese, to serve

Prep time 5 minutes | **Cook time** 10 minutes |
Calorie count 518 calories per portion

Spray a large frying pan (skillet) with some low-calorie cooking spray and place over a medium heat. Add the onion and garlic and fry for 2 minutes until softened.

Meanwhile, put the grated potato into the centre of a clean tea towel. Fold the towel around the potato and squeeze out the excess moisture over the sink.

Add the grated potato to the pan with the salt and pepper and smoked paprika and fry for 3 minutes so they get slightly crispy. Add the pork and dried sage, along with the cherry tomatoes and spinach leaves. Cook for about 5 minutes, stirring regularly and breaking up the mince with a wooden spoon.

Move the potato and sausage mixture to one side of the pan, then crack the eggs into the other half. Mix them up until they start to scramble, then gradually mix them into the sausage mixture until mixed through evenly. Remove from the heat, sprinkle over the feta to serve.

Note If not eating 2 portions, this is just as delicious when refrigerated and reheated – it will keep for up to 5 days.

MID-WEEK

MEALS

Mondays often start off with the best intentions in the world: it's a new week, a new start, and the day when people most often start their healthy-eating mindset or diet. I personally find that Tuesdays are often harder to deal with than Mondays as the motivation slowly starts to dwindle, but by the time Wednesday hits, we just want the week to be over already as the end is in sight.

For years I have been creating 'weeknight recipes' that I shared on my socials and website on a Wednesday. This chapter is based on that idea: simple, delicious meals that can be prepared or cooked in just 15 minutes, making them perfect for weekday cooking when your motivation to get in the kitchen and prepare a fresh meal is low.

This doesn't mean that you need to sacrifice any of the taste, though - if you were served one of these meals you would never know just how quickly it was prepared.

The recipes are all created using ingredients that you should already have in the house, or can easily get from your local supermarket, with no faff or frills.

Check out some of my tips in the introduction to help you speed up the cooking process even more.

lemon and courgette orzo

This tasty, creamy vegetarian orzo recipe has a lovely lemony kick. It is great as a meal to prep ahead too, and can be kept in the refrigerator for meals throughout the week. The orzo can be replaced with other small pasta shapes as well.

MAKES 4 PORTIONS

250g (9oz) orzo
½ onion, finely diced
165g (5¾oz) low-fat cream
    cheese
1 large courgette
    (zucchini), cut into thin
    strips (I use a vegetable
    peeler to do this)
Juice of 1 lemon
Low-calorie cooking spray
Sea salt and freshly ground
    black pepper

Prep time 5 minutes | **Cook time** 10 minutes | **Calorie count** 380 calories per portion

Par-cook the orzo in a saucepan of salted boiling water for 5 minutes.

Meanwhile, spray a large frying pan (skillet) with some low-calorie cooking spray and place over a medium heat. Add the onion and cook for 5 minutes until softened, then add the cream cheese and a few tablespoons of cooking water from the orzo pan.

Drain the par-cooked orzo, then add it to the frying pan along with the courgette strips and the lemon juice. Season with salt and pepper, mix well and cook for a further 5 minutes. You should have a creamy sauce and the orzo should be fully cooked.

Note This dish can be split into portions and refrigerated for up to 5 days. Reheat fully before serving.

creamy tomato vodka pasta

If you have my book *Slimming & Tasty*, you will have seen a delicious tomato and vodka soup recipe. Tomato and vodka is a traditional Italian-American flavour combination, and a similar pasta dish went viral in 2022. This healthier twist has become very popular on my blog!

Prep time 5 minutes | **Cook time** 10 minutes | **Calorie count** 370 calories per portion

MAKES 4 PORTIONS

200g (7oz) dried penne pasta
1 red onion, finely diced
1 garlic clove, diced
2 tablespoons tomato purée (paste)
100g (3½oz) low-fat cream cheese
1 tablespoon vodka
¼ red chilli, finely diced
60g (2¼oz) grated Parmesan
Low-calorie cooking spray
Sea salt and freshly ground black pepper

Cook the pasta in a pan of salted boiling water according to the packet instructions.

Meanwhile, spray a large frying pan (skillet) with some low-calorie cooking spray and place over a medium heat. Add the onion and garlic and cook for 3 minutes until softened, then stir in the tomato purée. Add the cream cheese and stir until melted, then add the vodka, stir and cook for a further 5 minutes. Add the chilli and stir until combined, season with salt and pepper and remove from the heat.

When the pasta is cooked, save a quarter of the pasta cooking water before draining. Add the drained pasta and the pasta cooking water to the sauce and stir well to combine. Season with more salt and pepper and serve with the Parmesan sprinkled on top.

Notes The vodka helps bind the ingredients together and softens the tanginess of the tomatoes to make a creamy sauce. You cook off the alcohol, so don't worry about getting tipsy from this tasty dish!

The dish can be refrigerated for up to 5 days. Reheat fully before serving.

creamy tuscan-style mixed bean stew

This recipe is so filling and comforting, I love making it in the winter. It is vegan too, so perfect for any meat-free day. The creaminess comes from coconut milk here – it's not strictly Tuscan, but it adds such a yummy flavour.

MAKES 4 PORTIONS

1 small red onion, diced
1 garlic clove, minced
1 x 400g (14oz) tin of
   cannellini beans, drained
1 x 400g (14oz) tin of
   kidney beans, drained
Handful of spinach leaves,
   roughly chopped
4 sun-dried tomatoes, cut
   into small bite-sized
   pieces
100ml (3½fl oz/scant ½ cup)
   vegetable stock
3 tablespoons light coconut
   milk
Low-calorie cooking spray
Sea salt and freshly ground
   black pepper

Prep time 2 minutes | **Cook time** 13 minutes | **Calorie count** 376 calories per portion

Spray a frying pan (skillet) with some low-calorie cooking spray and place over a medium heat. Add the onion and garlic and fry for 2 minutes, then add both tins of beans, the spinach, sun-dried tomatoes and stock. Season with a pinch each of salt and pepper, reduce the heat and simmer for 10 minutes.

Finally, stir through the coconut milk until warmed through and serve.

Note This stew can be refrigerated for up to 5 days. Reheat fully before serving.

garlic mushroom gnocchi

This tasty vegetarian recipe is based on the flavours of garlic mushrooms. I love garlic mushrooms and could eat this dish every day! It is made with ready-made gnocchi. Gnocchi are potato dumplings that you can buy in most supermarkets.

MAKES 4 PORTIONS

1 x 500g (1lb 2oz) pack of gnocchi

1 onion, finely diced

200g (7oz) closed-cup mushrooms, thinly sliced

3 garlic cloves, finely diced

1 teaspoon dried parsley

120g (4¼oz) low-fat cream cheese

½ teaspoon wholegrain mustard

Low-calorie cooking spray

Sea salt and freshly ground black pepper

Prep time 5 minutes | **Cook time** 10 minutes | **Calorie count** 430 calories per portion

Cook the gnocchi in a pan of salted boiling water according to the packet instructions.

Meanwhile, spray a frying pan (skillet) with some low-calorie cooking spray and place over a medium heat. Add the onion and cook for 2 minutes until softened, then stir in the mushrooms before adding the garlic. Cook for a further 3 minutes, being careful not to burn the garlic. Add the parsley, cream cheese and mustard, season with salt and pepper and stir until the cream cheese has melted. Add 2 tablespoons of the gnocchi cooking water to the sauce and stir until smooth and creamy. Add more water if required, to help form a sauce.

Drain the gnocchi, add it to the sauce and mix until it is coated in the creamy sauce. Serve.

Note This dish can be refrigerated for up to 5 days. Reheat fully before serving.

pepperoni pizza macaroni

This delicious recipe is inspired by pepperoni pizza flavours and is so simple to make, and the melted mozzarella on top makes this just like a pizza topping! The whole family will love it.

MAKES 4 PORTIONS

250g (9oz) dried macaroni

1 onion, finely diced

2 garlic cloves, finely diced

1 red (bell) pepper, deseeded and finely diced

45g (1½oz) sliced pepperoni

1 x 400g (14oz) tin of chopped tomatoes

1 teaspoon dried basil

1 teaspoon smoked paprika

Pinch each of sea salt and freshly ground black pepper

1 beef stock cube

160g (5½oz) reduced-fat grated mozzarella

Low-calorie cooking spray

Prep time 5 minutes | **Cook time** 15 minutes | **Calorie count** 460 calories per portion

Par-cook the macaroni in a saucepan of salted boiling water for 5–6 minutes.

Meanwhile, spray a large frying pan (skillet) with some low-calorie cooking spray and place over a medium heat. Add the onion and fry for 2 minutes until softened, then add the garlic and red pepper and fry for a further 2 minutes.

Slice 3 of the pepperoni slices, add them to the pan and stir, then add the chopped tomatoes, basil, paprika, salt and pepper. Crumble in the stock cube, reduce the heat to low and simmer for 5 minutes.

Drain the macaroni, add it to the frying pan and stir it through the sauce, then simmer for 5 minutes.

Take the pan off the heat and top with the mozzarella and the rest of the pepperoni slices. Place the pan under a hot grill (broiler) until the cheese is bubbling.

~~~~

Notes This works well with any smaller pasta shape.

To make this dish vegetarian, omit the pepperoni and use vegetable stock.

This recipe works best if you have a metal-handled frying pan that you can put under a hot grill at the end.

spiced red daal with garlic flatbreads

Daal is a thick, spicy Indian lentil stew – and my version is vegan. You have control over how spicy you make it, but I enjoy mine when it has a bit of bite. The daal is perfect for freezing as well. The garlic flatbreads are absolutely perfect for dipping into the daal!

Prep time 5 minutes | **Cook time** 15 minutes | **Calorie count** 535 calories per portion

MAKES 2 PORTIONS

1 green chilli, deseeded and finely diced (adjust to taste)
2 garlic cloves, finely diced
1 teaspoon 'lazy' ginger from a jar (or a thumb-sized piece of fresh ginger, finely diced)
2 teaspoons ground cumin
½ onion, thinly sliced
1 x 400g (14oz) tin of chopped tomatoes
Pinch of sea salt
200g (7oz) dried red lentils, rinsed in a sieve until the water runs clear
400ml (14fl oz/1⅔ cups) boiling water
½ teaspoon ground turmeric
Low-calorie cooking spray

For the flatbreads

100g (3½oz/½ cup) self-raising (self-rising) flour, plus extra for dusting
80g (2¾oz) fat-free Greek yoghurt
1 teaspoon garlic granules
1 teaspoon finely chopped parsley leaves

Mix together the ingredients for the flatbreads until they combine to form a dough. Tip onto a floured surface and knead for a minute or two until smooth. Split into 4 balls and set aside while you prepare the daal.

Spray a saucepan with some low-calorie cooking spray and place over a medium heat. Add the chilli, garlic, ginger and cumin and fry for a few minutes, then add the sliced onion, chopped tomatoes and salt. Add the rinsed and drained lentils to the saucepan, followed by the boiling water and the turmeric. Bring to the boil, then reduce the heat and simmer for about 10 minutes until the lentils are soft and the liquid has thickened.

While that is cooking away, spray a frying pan (skillet) with low-calorie cooking spray and place over a high heat. Flatten out one of the flatbread balls with your hands or a rolling pin to a thickness of roughly 1 cm (½ inch), then cook in the hot pan on each side for 30 seconds, until cooked through and browned. Repeat with the remaining flatbreads.

Note This daal freezes well for up to 1 month, or can be refrigerated for 5 days. Reheat fully before serving.

feta, veg and new potato traybake

This recipe is one of my favourite ways to make a meal: just throw everything in a dish and let it cook! It's a twist on the feta pasta trend, but a lower-carb version. The preparation time is just so speedy!

MAKES 2 PORTIONS

1 courgette (zucchini),
  roughly chopped
1 x 200g (7oz) block of
  reduced-fat feta cheese,
  cut into cubes
1 red onion, cut into wedges
200g (7oz) new potatoes,
  quartered
250g (9oz) cherry tomatoes,
  halved
2 red (bell) peppers,
  deseeded and thinly
  sliced
1 tablespoon balsamic
  vinegar
1 garlic clove, diced
Pinch each of sea salt and
  black pepper
½ teaspoon dried chilli (hot
  red pepper) flakes
Low-calorie cooking spray

Prep time 5 minutes | **Cook time** 15 minutes | **Calorie count** 350 calories per portion

Preheat the oven to 200°C/180°C fan/400°F/Gas mark 6.

Put all of the ingredients in an ovenproof dish and spray with low-calorie cooking spray. Bake in the oven for 15 minutes, or until the potatoes are cooked through and browned.

Remove, stir to mix the ingredients together and serve.

Note This dish can be refrigerated for up to 5 days. Reheat fully before serving.

BBQ chicken rice

My famous BBQ flavours are the star of the show in this recipe, with succulent chicken and a lovely sticky rice. I know that this will be a firm family favourite to all who make it!

MAKES 4 PORTIONS

1 red onion, diced

1 red (bell) pepper, deseeded and sliced

1 yellow (bell) pepper, deseeded and sliced

500g (1lb 2oz) skinless, boneless chicken breast, diced

2 tablespoons Worcestershire sauce

2 teaspoons balsamic vinegar

2 garlic cloves, crushed

1 teaspoon English mustard powder

2 teaspoons smoked paprika

Handful of frozen peas

100g (3½oz) tinned sweetcorn

1 celery stick, finely chopped

1 vegetable stock cube, dissolved in 125ml (4¼fl oz/generous ½ cup) water

1 x 500g (1lb 2oz) carton of passata (sieved tomatoes)

¼ teaspoon red chilli powder

2 x 220g (7¾oz) packs of microwave rice

Low-calorie cooking spray

Sea salt and freshly ground black pepper

Prep time 10 minutes | **Cook time** 15 minutes |
Calorie count 420 calories per portion

Spray a large frying pan (skillet) with some low-calorie cooking spray and place over a medium heat. Add the onion and peppers and fry for 5 minutes, then add the chicken, Worcestershire sauce and balsamic vinegar. Stir and cook for 5 minutes, then add the garlic, mustard powder, smoked paprika, peas, sweetcorn and celery and fry for a few minutes until the celery has softened.

Add the stock, passata and chilli powder, season with salt and pepper, and cook for a further 2 minutes, then stir in the cooked rice, mixing well to ensure it is fully coated in all the flavours. Cook for 2 minutes until the rice has changed colour and has a slightly sticky consistency.

Note I use microwave rice to help with time saving, but this could be replaced with cooked rice.

spicy lime and prawn tacos

I love a taco: it is such a quick and easy dinner to prepare. This recipe combines spicy prawns with a citrussy freshness. It makes 2 tacos per person and works perfectly with mini tortilla wraps which you can buy in most supermarkets.

MAKES 2 PORTIONS
(2 TACOS PER PORTION)

1 garlic clove, finely
    chopped
200g (7oz) raw shelled
    prawns (shrimp)
1 red chilli, deseeded and
    finely chopped
Juice of 1 lime
Low-calorie cooking spray
Sea salt and freshly ground
    black pepper

For the smoky paprika sauce

3 tablespoons fat-free Greek
    yoghurt
1 teaspoon smoked paprika
Pinch each of sea salt and
    freshly ground black
    pepper

To serve

50g (1¾oz) iceberg lettuce,
    chopped
A few coriander (cilantro)
    leaves, finely chopped
4 mini tortilla wraps
Lime wedges

Prep time 5 minutes | **Cook time** 7 minutes |
Calorie count 400 calories per portion

Spray a frying pan (skillet) with some low-calorie cooking spray and place over a medium heat. Add the garlic, prawns and chilli and cook for 3–4 minutes, or until the prawns have turned pink. Season with salt and pepper and drizzle with the lime juice, then remove from the heat.

Mix together the sauce ingredients together in a bowl.

Assemble the lettuce, prawns and coriander on one half of each of the mini tortilla wraps. Add a dollop of paprika sauce, then fold over and serve with lime wedges for squeezing.

Notes This recipe packs a spicy punch, but you can adjust this to suit your taste by using less chilli.

To make these tacos dairy free, use dairy-free yoghurt.

crispy garlic and parmesan chicken breasts with vegetable rice

This is a truly scrumptious way to enjoy chicken and is so simple to prepare too. It also works well if you want to prep the chicken ahead of time and refrigerate it until you're ready to cook it. I like to serve this with rice and greens or a fresh and crunchy salad.

MAKES 2 PORTIONS

2 large skinless, boneless
   chicken breasts
1 egg
1 x 250g (9oz) pack
   of microwave golden
   vegetable rice, to serve

For the crumb coating

2 slices of wholemeal bread
2 tablespoons grated
   Parmesan
1 garlic clove, finely diced
1 teaspoon dried parsley
Pinch each of sea salt and
   freshly ground black
   pepper

Prep time 10 minutes | **Cook time** 20 minutes | **Calorie count** 489 calories per portion

Preheat the oven to 200°C/180°C fan/400°F/Gas mark 6 and line a baking tray (sheet) with baking parchment.

Put the crumb coating ingredients in a food processor and blitz until combined to form a crumb.

Meanwhile, put the chicken breasts between two sheets of cling film (plastic wrap), then use a rolling pin to bash them until they are thinner and about half their original thickness.

Crack the egg into a shallow bowl and beat it. Put the crumb coating into a separate shallow bowl. Dip the flattened breasts into the egg, then into the breadcrumb mixture. Repeat twice, if necessary, to completely coat the breasts.

Place on the lined baking tray and then cook in the oven for 20 minutes until the coating is crisp and the chicken is cooked through.

Serve with the rice.

~~~

Notes The key to making this recipe speedy is flattening out the chicken breast so that it cooks quicker.

The breasts can also be air fried at 200°C for 10 minutes.

To make this gluten free, use gluten-free bread.

cheeky piri piri chicken one-pan wonder

Inspired by the flavours of the popular 'cheeky' chicken high-street brand, the beauty of this dish is that there is very little preparation: you can throw everything into the oven in one dish and let it do all the work for you.

MAKES 4 PORTIONS

1 red (bell) pepper,
   deseeded and thinly
   sliced
1 x 250g (9oz) pack of
   microwave long-grain rice
300g (10½oz) frozen peas
250g (9oz) skinless,
   boneless chicken breasts,
   diced
150g (5½oz) halloumi,
   thinly sliced

For the peri-peri sauce

2 red chillies (adjust
   according to how much
   you like spice!)
1 red (bell) pepper, halved
   and deseeded
1 red onion, halved
1 tablespoon smoked paprika
2 teaspoons salt
1 teaspoon freshly ground
   black pepper
1 tablespoon dried oregano
½ teaspoon red chilli powder
4 garlic cloves
4 tablespoons malt vinegar
8 cherry tomatoes
Juice of 1 lemon
Juice of ½ lime

Prep time 5 minutes | **Cook time** 15 minutes | **Calorie count** 450 calories per portion

Blitz all the ingredients for the sauce in a food processor or blender with 50ml (1¾fl oz/3½ tablespoons) water until smooth.

Pour the sauce into an ovenproof dish, add the sliced red pepper, microwave rice and peas and mix. Add the diced chicken on top, then the sliced halloumi. Cook for 10 minutes, remove and stir everything together, then return to the oven for a further 5 minutes until the chicken is cooked through.

Note The cooked dish can be refrigerated for up to 2 days. Reheat fully before serving.

chicken and mushroom stroganoff

My beef stroganoff is a huge hit on my website, and in my book *Slimming & Tasty*, and this is my speedy chicken version. The sauce is so deliciously creamy, you would never know that it has fewer calories than a regular stroganoff. It can be served with rice, pasta or potatoes.

MAKES 2 PORTIONS

500g (1lb 2oz) skinless, boneless chicken breast, diced

2 teaspoons Worcestershire sauce

1 teaspoon white wine vinegar

1 onion, finely diced

200g (7oz) button mushrooms, thinly sliced

1 teaspoon English mustard powder

100ml (3½fl oz/scant ½ cup) chicken stock

200g (7oz) low-fat cream cheese

Low-calorie cooking spray

Sea salt and freshly ground black pepper

Parsley leaves, to serve

Prep time 5 minutes | **Cook time** 15 minutes | **Calorie count** 350 calories per portion

Spray a large frying pan (skillet) with some low-calorie cooking spray and place over a medium heat. Add the diced chicken, season with salt and pepper and cook for 5 minutes.

Add the Worcestershire sauce and white wine vinegar, then the onion and mushrooms and cook for a further 5 minutes before adding the mustard powder and the stock to the pan. Reduce the heat to low, stir in the cream cheese and cook for 5 minutes until smooth and creamy (making sure the chicken is cooked through). Serve sprinkled with parsley.

Notes To make this dish vegetarian, use tofu or a meat-free alternative (and swap the chicken stock for vegetable stock).

Refrigerate for up to 3 days. Reheat fully before serving.

chicken fajita pasta

I love fajitas, I always used to get so excited when Mum would say we were having them for dinner. This pasta has all the familiar delicious flavours, and the creaminess of the sauce balances out the spicy kick.

MAKES 4 PORTIONS

250g (9oz) dried pasta

1 red (bell) pepper, deseeded and finely chopped

1 yellow (bell) pepper, deseeded and finely chopped

1 red onion, diced

2 large skinless, boneless chicken breasts, diced

1 teaspoon smoked paprika

1 teaspoon ground cumin

1 fresh red chilli, deseeded and finely chopped

1 teaspoon red chilli powder

Juice of 1 lime

1 garlic clove, crushed

1 tablespoon tomato purée (paste)

1 x 500g (1lb 2oz) carton of passata (sieved tomatoes)

2 tablespoons low-fat cream cheese

80g (2¾oz) reduced-fat Cheddar cheese, grated, to serve

Low-calorie cooking spray

Sea salt and freshly ground black pepper

For the optional topping

30g (1oz) crushed spicy tortilla chips (149 extra calories total, 37 calories per portion)

Prep time 5 minutes | **Cook time** 15 minutes | **Calorie count** 450 calories per portion

Cook the pasta in a saucepan of salted boiling water according to the packet instructions.

Spray a frying pan (skillet) with some low-calorie cooking spray and place over a medium heat. Add the peppers and onion and cook for 2 minutes, then add the diced chicken along with the smoked paprika, cumin, fresh chilli, chilli powder, lime juice, garlic and tomato purée. Season with salt and pepper and fry for 8 minutes until the chicken is cooked through.

Add the passata and the cream cheese and a couple of tablespoons of the pasta cooking water, then simmer for 2–3 minutes.

Drain the pasta and add it to the sauce, stir well and top with the cheese and tortilla chips (if using).

Note Can be refrigerated for up to 5 days. Reheat fully before serving.

sticky turkey meatballs

A delicious Asian-inspired turkey mince recipe that's really easy to make, and extremely delicious! Meatballs can be boring in the same old tomato sauce, which is why I think you'll love this recipe. The meatballs have a sticky sweet sauce that takes them to the next level. Try them served with noodles or rice.

MAKES 2 PORTIONS

500g (1lb 2oz) extra-lean 5%-fat minced (ground) turkey
1 tablespoon fat-free Greek yoghurt
Low-calorie cooking spray
Sea salt and freshly ground black pepper

For the sauce

4 tablespoons rice vinegar
2 tablespoons honey
2 garlic cloves, minced
4 tablespoons low-sodium soy sauce
1 teaspoon toasted sesame oil
1 teaspoon ground ginger

To serve

1 teaspoon white sesame seeds
Chopped spring onions (scallions)

Prep time 10 minutes | **Cook time** 15 minutes | **Calorie count** 400 calories per portion

Preheat the oven to 200°C/180°C fan/400°F/Gas mark 6 and spray a baking tray (sheet) with some low-calorie cooking spray.

In a bowl, mix together the turkey and yoghurt with your hands, seasoning well with salt and pepper. Roll the mixture into small, evenly-sized meatballs and lay them out onto the greased tray. Bake in the oven for 15 minutes, or until the balls are cooked through.

Meanwhile, put all the sauce ingredients into a saucepan and bring to the boil, stirring regularly. Reduce the heat and simmer over a low heat for 10 minutes, or until the sauce has reduced and thickened.

Once the meatballs are ready, add them to the sauce and gently toss them to coat them evenly in the sauce. Sprinkle with the sesame seeds and chopped spring onions (scallions) to serve.

Note The meatballs and sauce can be refrigerated for up to 5 days (or frozen, without the sauce). Reheat fully before serving.

cajun-style turkey, courgette and pepper rice

I love a one-pan recipe, and this one has a delicious Cajun-inspired flavour. The sauce has a lovely kick from the sriracha and is a super filling and easy mid-week meal. Having the leftovers of this dish the next day for lunch is such a treat.

MAKES 4 PORTIONS

1 large courgette (zucchini), finely diced

1 garlic clove, minced

2 red (bell) peppers, deseeded and sliced

1 teaspoon 'lazy' ginger (or a thumbnail-sized piece of fresh ginger, grated)

500g (1lb 2oz) extra-lean 5%-fat minced (ground) turkey

1 x 220g (7¾oz) pack of microwave basmati rice

Low-calorie cooking spray

A few spring onions (scallions), chopped, to serve

For the sauce

3 tablespoons teriyaki sauce

2 tablespoons dark soy sauce

2 tablespoons sriracha sauce

For the Cajun spice mix

3 teaspoons smoked paprika

1 teaspoon garlic granules

1 teaspoon ground white pepper

1 teaspoon onion powder

1 teaspoon dried oregano

1 teaspoon cayenne pepper

Prep time 10 minutes | **Cook time** 10 minutes | **Calorie count** 380 calories per portion

Prepare the sauce by mixing together the ingredients in a bowl. If it looks a little too thick, add a tablespoon or so of water.

Combine the spice mix ingredients in a bowl.

Spray a large frying pan (skillet) with some low-calorie cooking spray and place over a medium heat. Add the courgette, garlic, red peppers and ginger and fry for 2 minutes, then add the turkey and the spice mix and fry for 6 minutes, breaking up the mince with a wooden spoon, until browned. Pour over the sauce and mix well.

Cook the rice according to the packet instructions, then add it to the turkey mixture. Mix well, then serve with some chopped spring onions on top.

Note I use microwave rice to help make this speedy, but this could be replaced with cooked rice.

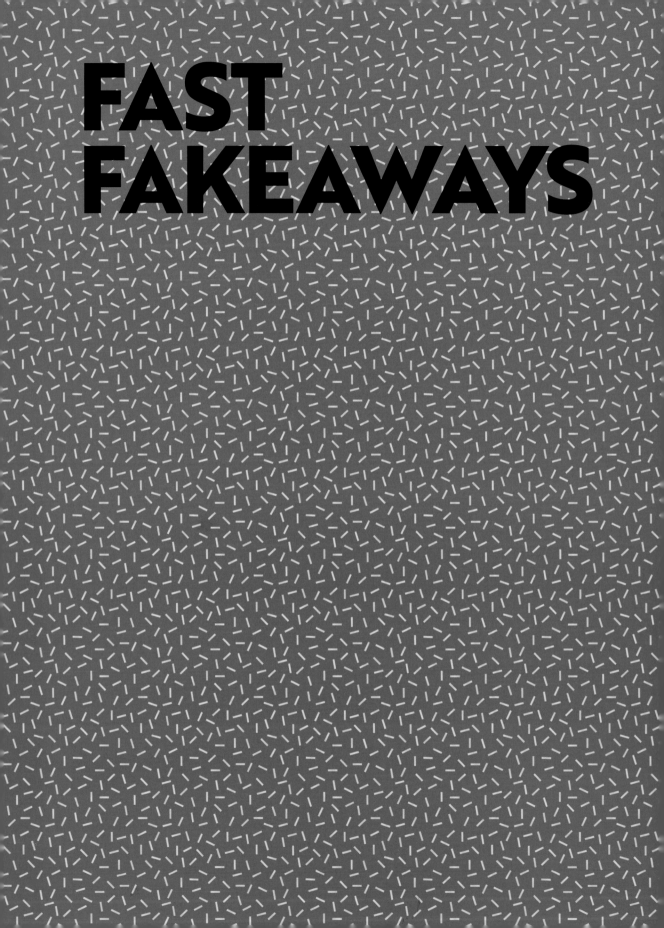

FAST
FAKEAWAYS

Have I mentioned that I am the 'Queen of the Fakeaway'? That's what the papers say, anyway… If you haven't heard of a fakeaway before, imagine your favourite dishes from the takeaway, but made at home. When preparing something freshly at home, you can manage exactly the amount of sugar and oil you use, meaning that it is healthier too. Not only are there health benefits, but often you will find it is much cheaper to make your own feast at home.

I started making fakeaways to learn how to recreate healthier versions of some of my favourite dishes at home, as I love the challenge and learning how to cook new cuisines.

Back in 2020, at the height of the pandemic, I went viral with my fakeaway recipes. I was interviewed by TV and radio about my recipes, with lots of mainstream media sharing them. It was mad to see.

One thing that traditional takeaways do have in their favour is that they require a lot less effort and time. Just a few clicks or a call and you can get something delivered or collected.

That's where my 'fast fakeaways' come in! I have put together a selection of low-calorie takeaway favourites that can be either cooked or prepped in just 15 minutes! This means less effort and maximum enjoyment, plus you have the satisfaction of knowing you made it all yourself!

chicken wings three ways

These wings are perfect cooked in an air fryer, but are just as tasty when oven-baked too! With 3 flavours to choose from, you will never get bored of these delicious wings. The baking powder helps to make the wings crispy without the need to deep-fry them.

I've included two sauced wings here. Buffalo is a buttery, spicy sauce from the US that is a classic wing flavour. When I visited London recently I found an incredible Korean street-food vendor in one of the food markets and adored their Korean chicken wings, so I had to have a go at recreating the flavours myself at home!

Try serving these wings with the Ranch Dip on page 195.

original american-style chicken wings

MAKES 2 PORTIONS
500g (1lb 2oz) chicken wings
Low-calorie cooking spray

For the spice rub
1 teaspoon smoked paprika
½ teaspoon red chilli powder
1 teaspoon garlic granules
½ teaspoon onion powder
1 chicken stock cube, crumbled
Pinch each of sea salt and freshly ground black pepper
1 teaspoon baking powder

Prep time 5 minutes | **Cook time** 15 minutes |
Calorie count 230 calories per portion

Set the air fryer to 200°C (or, if using an oven, preheat it to 200°C/180°C fan/400°F/Gas mark 6).

Mix the ingredients for the spice rub together in a bowl, then toss in the wings and mix well to coat them evenly in the spices.

Spray the air-fryer tray with low-calorie cooking spray, then lay out the wings. Spray with a little more cooking spray and cook in the air fryer for 15 minutes, turning them halfway through, until they are thoroughly cooked and crispy and browned on the outside. (If oven cooking, lay the wings out on a baking sheet and cook for 20 minutes.)

Note If you don't like wings, these flavours work just as well with sliced chicken breast.

buffalo chicken wings

MAKES 2 PORTIONS
500g (1lb 2oz) chicken wings
Low-calorie cooking spray
Celery sticks, to serve

For the seasoning mix
1 teaspoon smoked paprika
1 teaspoon cayenne pepper
1 teaspoon garlic granules
2 teaspoons baking powder
Pinch each of sea salt and
   freshly ground black
   pepper

For the sauce
2 tablespoons Worcestershire
   sauce
1 tablespoon sriracha sauce
½ tablespoon honey

Prep time 5 minutes | **Cook time** 10 minutes |
Calorie count 280 calories per portion

Set the air fryer to 200°C (or, if using an oven, preheat it to 200°C/180°C fan/400°F/Gas mark 6).

Mix the ingredients for the seasoning mix together in a bowl, then toss in the wings and mix well to coat them evenly in the spices.

Spray the air-fryer tray with low-calorie cooking spray, then lay out the wings. Spray with a little more cooking spray and cook in the air fryer for 15 minutes, turning them halfway through. (If oven cooking, lay the wings out on a baking sheet and cook for 20 minutes.)

While the wings are cooking, combine the sauce ingredients in a small saucepan over a low heat, mixing well.

When the wings are cooked, pour the sauce all over and mix well. Serve immediately with celery sticks.

Note If you like spice, add a little more cayenne pepper!

korean-style chicken wings

MAKES 2 PORTIONS

500g (1lb 2oz) chicken wings
Low-calorie cooking spray

For the sauce

2 tablespoons low-fat butter
   spread
1 tablespoon gochujang
2 tablespoons light soy
   sauce
1 tablespoon minced garlic
1 teaspoon 'lazy' ginger
   from a jar (or a thumb-
   sized piece of fresh
   ginger, grated)
2 tablespoons honey
1 tablespoon rice vinegar
1 teaspoon toasted sesame
   oil

To serve

White sesame seeds
Chopped spring onions
   (scallions)

Prep time 5 minutes | **Cook time** 15 minutes |
Calorie count 230 calories per portion

Set the air fryer to 200°C (or, if using an oven, preheat it to
200°C/180°C fan/400°F/Gas mark 6).

Put all the ingredients for the sauce in a saucepan with
2 tablespoons water and simmer over a low heat for 5 minutes
until the sauce has thickened slightly.

Spray the air-fryer tray with low-calorie cooking spray, then lay
out the wings. Spray with a little more cooking spray and cook
in the air fryer for 15 minutes, turning them halfway through. (If
oven cooking, lay the wings out on a baking sheet and cook for
20 minutes.)

When the wings are cooked, toss them in the sauce and sprinkle
with sesame seeds and spring onions to serve.

Note Gochujang, a red Korean chilli paste,
is available at most supermarkets.

naan bread pizza

This is a super yummy naan bread-based pizza – pizza with an Indian twist! The topping possibilities are endless with this, but this is my personal favourite flavour combination, with a little spice and sweetness. Serve with a big side salad.

Prep time 5 minutes | **Cook time** 12 minutes | **Calorie count** 535 calories per pizza

MAKES 2 PIZZAS

125g (4¼oz) baby spinach leaves
100g (3½oz) passata (sieved tomatoes)
1 tablespoon tikka curry powder (or any curry powder)
2 plain mini naans (47g/1⅔oz each)
110g (3¾oz) reduced-fat mozzarella
80g (2¾oz) reduced-fat mature Cheddar cheese, grated
½ red onion, thinly sliced
Juice of 1 lemon

Preheat the oven to 200°C/180°C fan/400°F/Gas mark 6.

Put the spinach in a pan of hot water and let it sit for 2–3 minutes until wilted, then drain and squeeze out any excess water.

Mix the passata with the tikka curry powder until combined. Spread the mixture over the naans, then tear the mozzarella and add it to the top of each naan bread. Sprinkle with the grated Cheddar, then the sliced red onion and spinach, then drizzle with the lemon juice.

Bake in the oven for 12 minutes, until the cheese is melted and bubbling.

soy, garlic and chilli noodles

Perfect for a weeknight fakeaway, this dish is full of flavour and so easy that even the most unconfident cooks can prepare it. It takes only 15 minutes to make, from start to finish, including the prep time!

MAKES 4 PORTIONS

2 x 50g (1¾oz) nests of
   dried egg noodles
1 onion, thinly sliced
2 garlic cloves, minced
1 red chilli, deseeded and
   finely chopped
2 teaspoons 'lazy' ginger
   from a jar (or a generous
   thumb-sized piece of
   fresh ginger, grated)
3 spring onions (scallions),
   finely chopped
4 tablespoons low-sodium
   soy sauce
1 tablespoon honey
1 tablespoon sriracha sauce
2 teaspoons rice vinegar
1 tablespoon toasted
   sesame oil
4 medium eggs
Low-calorie cooking spray
Chopped spring onions
   (scallions), to serve

Prep time 5 minutes | **Cook time** 10 minutes | **Calorie count** 405 calories per portion

Cook the noodles in a saucepan of boiling water according to the packet instructions.

Spray a saucepan or wok with some low-calorie cooking spray and place over a medium heat. Add the onion, garlic, chilli, ginger and spring onions and stir-fry for 3 minutes, then add the soy sauce, honey, sriracha, vinegar and sesame oil and mix well to combine. Reduce the heat.

Drain the cooked noodles, add them to the pan or wok and fry for 2 minutes. Mix well until they are coated evenly in the sauce then remove from the heat while you cook the eggs.

Spray a frying pan (skillet) with some low-calorie cooking spray, place over a medium heat and add the eggs. Cover with a lid and cook for 3 minutes, or until the white is set.

Serve the egg on top of the noodles, and sprinkle with the spring onions.

sticky whiskey chicken strips

This fakeaway is inspired by the restaurant brand that is a big fan of a Friday! The sticky strips of chicken with a BBQ glaze, topped with sesame seeds, can be served as a tasty starter but I really enjoy them served with a salad.

MAKES 2 PORTIONS

1 large egg, beaten

2 slices of wholemeal bread, blitzed in a blender to make breadcrumbs

1 teaspoon sweet paprika

¾ teaspoon sea salt

½ teaspoon garlic granules

2 teaspoons white sesame seeds

2 large skinless, boneless chicken breasts, cut into strips

Low-calorie cooking spray

Salad, to serve

For the BBQ glaze

1 onion, finely diced

2 large garlic cloves, finely diced

2 tablespoons pineapple juice

120ml (4fl oz) teriyaki sauce

2 tablespoons dark soy sauce

6 tablespoons lemon juice

5 teaspoons cider vinegar

1 teaspoon red wine vinegar

2 tablespoons Jack Daniel's Whiskey (optional)

¼ teaspoon cayenne pepper

3 tablespoons granulated sweetener

Prep time 10 minutes | **Cook time** 20 minutes | **Calorie count** 440 calories per portion

Preheat the oven to 200°C/180°C fan/400°F/Gas mark 6 and line a baking tray (sheet) with baking parchment.

First, make the BBQ glaze. Spray a saucepan with some low-calorie cooking spray and place over a medium heat. Add the diced onion and garlic and cook, stirring, for 2 minutes.

Combine the pineapple juice, teriyaki sauce, soy sauce, lemon juice, cider vinegar, red wine vinegar, whiskey and cayenne pepper in a bowl. Pour the liquid over the onion and garlic mixture and bring to the boil, stirring occasionally, then reduce the heat and add the sweetener. Simmer for 5 minutes until thickened and reduced by half.

Meanwhile, put the beaten egg in a shallow bowl. Mix the breadcrumbs, paprika, salt and garlic granules in a separate shallow bowl with half of the sesame seeds. Dip the chicken strips in the egg, then into the breadcrumb mix until coated.

Lay the coated strips out onto the lined tray, then spray with low-calorie cooking spray. Cook in the oven for 20 minutes, or until the chicken is cooked through.

When the chicken is ready, remove it from the oven and coat it fully in the glaze. Mix well, then sprinkle with the rest of the sesame seeds and serve with some salad.

Notes The whiskey is optional here but adds a nice kick.

These can be cooked in the air fryer too: set the air fryer to 200°C and cook for 15 minutes.

smash burgers

A smashed burger is a burger patty that you cook by pressing it down, or smashing if you will, with a spatula in the pan. I like to take it to the next level by frying some onions and pickles in the pan that you're cooking the burgers in so that some extra flavour gets 'smashed' into them. I also add the cheese to the burgers in the pan, then cover, so the cheese is really melted.

MAKES 2 BURGERS

½ red onion, very finely diced

2 pickled gherkins (dill pickles), very finely diced

40g (1½oz) reduced-fat Cheddar cheese, grated, per burger

Low-calorie cooking spray

For the burgers

250g (9oz) extra-lean 5%-fat minced (ground) beef

1 teaspoon smoked paprika

¼ teaspoon English mustard powder

Pinch each of sea salt and freshly ground black pepper

To serve

2 brioche buns

Lettuce

Prep time 10 minutes | **Cook time** 20 minutes | **Calorie count** 530 calories per burger

Combine the burger ingredients in a bowl. Split into 2 large balls, or 4 smaller balls if you want to make two double burgers.

Spray a heavy non-stick frying pan (skillet) with some low-calorie cooking spray and heat up for 5 minutes over a medium heat. Add the diced onion and gherkins and fry for 5 minutes, or until the onions have softened, then add the balls of burger mixture on top. Using a metal spatula, press down as hard as you can to form a thin, pressed-down burgers in the pan. Keep the spatula on each one for a minute and cook for 5 minutes, then flip the burgers and cook for a further 5 minutes. Add any excess onion and gherkins to the top of the burgers.

After the burgers have cooked for 5 minutes on their second side, top with the grated cheese. If you have a metal bowl, use it to cover the burgers in the pan so that the heat melts the cheese. Alternatively, cover the pan with a lid and cook for another 3 minutes.

Serve the burgers in a brioche bun with some lettuce.

Note This works best with a heavy cast-iron frying pan (skillet).

kung pao prawns

A deliciously spicy, stir-fried Chinese-style dish made with vegetables, prawns and nuts. This one-pan dish originally comes from the Sichuan area of China and is a really popular takeaway dish – this is my simple, low-calorie interpretation. Enjoy this on its own for a lower-carb option, but it's also delicious with noodles.

MAKES 2 PORTIONS

300g (10½oz) raw king prawns (shrimp), peeled and deveined
½ onion, finely chopped
1 red chilli, deseeded and finely diced
1 garlic clove, grated
2 teaspoons 'lazy' ginger from a jar (or a generous thumb-sized piece of fresh ginger, grated)
½ red (bell) pepper, deseeded and diced
½ green (bell) pepper, deseeded and diced
4 tablespoons toasted cashew nuts
A few spring onions (scallions), finely chopped
Low-calorie cooking spray

For the sauce

2 tablespoons light soy sauce
1 teaspoon dark soy sauce
1 tablespoon rice vinegar
1 tablespoon honey
1 teaspoon cornflour (cornstarch)
1 teaspoon toasted sesame oil

For the prawn seasoning

1 tablespoon light soy sauce
¼ teaspoon ground black pepper

Prep time 5 minutes | **Cook time** 15 minutes |
Calorie count 390 calories per portion

Whisk all the sauce ingredients in a bowl with 2 tablespoons water, then set aside.

Season the prawns with the soy sauce and pepper and set them aside until needed.

Spray a large frying pan (skillet) with some low-calorie cooking spray and place over a medium-high heat, then add the prawns and cook for 1–2 minutes. Once cooked, remove them from the heat and set them aside.

Spray the pan with some more low-calorie cooking spray, then add the onion and chilli and fry for 2 minutes. Add the garlic, ginger and peppers and cook for a few minutes, then add the cooked prawns back into the pan. Pour over the sauce and stir until it becomes thick, then remove from the heat and stir in the cashew nuts and spring onions.

sweet and sour chicken

I have a few different ways of making sweet and sour chicken, but this has to be the easiest and quickest way to create it. This is perfect for a weeknight fakeaway fix! Serve with rice or air-fried chips.

MAKES 4 PORTIONS

½ onion, thinly sliced

½ head of broccoli, cut into
    small florets

75g (2¾oz) mangetout,
    chopped in half

500g (1lb 2oz) skinless,
    boneless chicken breasts,
    cut into small chunks

½ teaspoon Chinese five-
    spice

Low-calorie cooking spray

For the sweet and sour sauce

2 tablespoons granulated
    sweetener

100ml (3½fl oz/scant ½ cup)
    cider vinegar

4 tablespoons tomato ketchup

2 tablespoons low-sodium soy
    sauce

1 teaspoon honey

1 tablespoon toasted
    sesame oil

3 garlic cloves, finely
    chopped

Pinch each of sea salt and
    freshly ground black
    pepper

1 tablespoon cornflour
    (cornstarch)

Prep time 5 minutes | **Cook time** 15 minutes |
Calorie count 475 calories per portion

Put all of the sauce ingredients, except the cornflour, in a medium saucepan and bring to the boil over a medium heat.

In a small bowl, combine the cornflour with 2 tablespoons water and mix to make a 'slurry' (I know it doesn't sound nice, but it does the job!). Add this to the sauce and stir until it thickens. Reduce the heat and let it simmer while you prepare the chicken.

Spray a frying pan (skillet) with some low-calorie cooking spray and place over a medium heat. Add the onion, broccoli and mangetout and fry for 2 minutes, then add the chicken and five-spice and fry for 5–10 minutes, until the chicken is cooked through.

Pour over the sauce and mix well until the chicken is coated.

Note To make this dish vegetarian, replace the chicken with Quorn or replica chicken.

crispy chilli beef fried rice

I've fused two takeaway favourites together here to make this easy, speedy, healthier version. This dish is made with beef mince, meaning it's quicker to prepare than whole cuts and as lean as possible, and I've combined it with the tasty sauce from a classic crispy chilli beef.

MAKES 4 PORTIONS

2 garlic cloves, finely chopped

½ teaspoon 'lazy' ginger from a jar (or a small piece of fresh ginger, grated)

500g (1lb 2oz) extra-lean 5%-fat minced (ground) beef

1 teaspoon onion salt

1 teaspoon Chinese five-spice

1 red chilli, deseeded and thinly sliced

1 tablespoon light soy sauce

1 tablespoon honey

Low-calorie cooking spray

For the fried rice

1 shallot, finely chopped

1 red (bell) pepper, deseeded and sliced

300g (10½oz) tinned and drained (or frozen) peas

500g (1lb 2oz) cooked, cold long-grain rice (or 2 x 220g/7¾oz packs of microwave rice, cooked)

2 tablespoons low-sodium soy sauce

1 tablespoon sriracha sauce

1 teaspoon Chinese five-spice

Prep time 2 minutes | **Cook time** 15 minutes | **Calorie count** 450 calories per portion

Firstly, prepare the crispy chilli beef. Spray a large frying pan (skillet) with some low-calorie cooking spray and place over a medium heat. Add the garlic and ginger and fry for 2 minutes, then add the beef and cook for 5 minutes or until the beef has browned, breaking up the mince with a wooden spoon as it cooks. Add the onion salt, five-spice and chilli, stir, then add the soy sauce and honey and stir until combined. Cook for a further 5 minutes: the beef should start to crisp up and the moisture evaporate. Once the beef is crispy, remove it from the pan and set it aside.

I cook the rice using the same pan I used for the beef, for extra flavour.

Spray it with a little more cooking spray, then add the shallot, red pepper and peas and cook for 1 minute over a medium heat. Add the cooked rice, soy sauce, sriracha and five-spice, mix well and fry for 2 minutes.

You can either add the crispy beef into the rice at this point and mix it before serving, or you can serve the rice with the crispy beef on top.

Note Replace the beef mince with soy mince to make this veggie.

thai red curry noodle bowl

I love Thai-style curries. In the UK, we eat green and red curry most often – if you've ever wondered what the difference is, other than the colour, it is down to the type of chillies used when making the dish. Red curry has a little bit more spice to it, thanks to the red chillies used in the curry paste.

MAKES 4 PORTIONS

1 level tablespoon Thai red
   curry paste
2 green chillies, deseeded
   and finely chopped
   (adjust to your preferred
   spice levels!)
1 onion, finely diced
1 red (bell) pepper,
   deseeded and finely diced
500g (1lb 2oz) skinless,
   boneless chicken breast,
   diced
1 x 400ml (14fl oz) tin of
   light coconut milk
400ml (14fl oz/1⅔ cups)
   chicken stock
2 x 50g (1¾oz) nests of
   dried egg noodles
Low-calorie cooking spray
Juice of 1 lime, to serve

Prep time 5 minutes | **Cook time** 15 minutes | **Calorie count** 455 calories per portion

Spray a large wok or saucepan with some low-calorie cooking spray and place over a high heat. Add the red curry paste, chillies, onion and pepper and stir-fry for 2–3 minutes, then add the chicken and cook for 5 minutes or until the chicken is browned all over. Add the coconut milk, stock and noodles, cover and simmer for 10 minutes, stirring occasionally.

Remove from the heat and squeeze over the lime juice to serve.

~~~~~

Note You can add any veggies you have in the fridge to this recipe!

coconut mushroom curry

A one-pan vegan wonder curry that is packed full of flavour. I love using chestnut mushrooms in this dish as they have a lovely rich taste, but any mushrooms will work well.

Prep time 5 minutes | **Cook time** 15 minutes | **Calorie count** 400 calories per portion

MAKES 4 PORTIONS

200g (7oz) baby button
    mushrooms
250g (9oz) chestnut
    mushrooms
1 onion, finely diced
2 garlic cloves, finely
    diced
1 tablespoon grated fresh
    ginger, or 1 teaspoon
    'lazy' ginger from a jar
2 tablespoons curry powder
1 x 400g (14oz) tin of
    chopped tomatoes
1 tablespoon tomato purée
    (paste)
200ml (7fl oz/scant 1 cup)
    light coconut milk
100ml (3½fl oz/scant ½ cup)
    vegetable stock
Juice of 1 lime
Low-calorie cooking spray
Sea salt and freshly ground
    black pepper

To serve
Chopped coriander (cilantro)
    leaves
2 x 220g (7¾oz) packs of
    microwave basmati rice

Spray a large saucepan or casserole dish with some low-calorie cooking spray and place over a medium heat. Add the mushrooms, onion, garlic and ginger and cook for 3 minutes until softened. Add the curry powder and stir for 1 minute, then add the chopped tomatoes, tomato purée, coconut milk and stock to the pan. Season with salt and pepper, reduce the heat and simmer for 10 minutes.

Just before serving, stir through the lime juice. Top with coriander and serve with rice.

Notes I like to cook this in my big cast-iron casserole dish (Dutch oven), but a large saucepan will do.

Refrigerate for up to 5 days. Reheat fully before serving.

butter chicken curry

Butter chicken is a lovely creamy curry with a warming spice. For my lower-calorie take I don't add as much butter as is typical in the traditional curry. Seasoning the chicken helps make it extra tasty! I like to serve it with rice.

MAKES 4 PORTIONS

For the spice mix

2 garlic cloves, crushed

1 teaspoon 'lazy' ginger from a jar (or a thumb-sized piece of fresh ginger, grated)

2 teaspoons red chilli powder

1 teaspoon sweet paprika

1 teaspoon garam masala

¼ teaspoon cayenne pepper

Pinch of sea salt

For the curry

4 skinless, boneless chicken breasts, diced

2 large onions, finely diced

200g (7oz) passata (sieved tomatoes)

1 vegetable stock cube, crumbled

2 tablespoons low-fat butter spread

3 tablespoons fat-free Greek yoghourt

Low-calorie cooking spray

Chopped coriander (cilantro) leaves, to serve

Prep time 5 minutes | **Cook time** 15 minutes | **Calorie count** 460 calories per portion

Combine the spice mix ingredients in a bowl, then halve the mix and set one half aside.

Add the diced chicken to half the spice mixture and mix until the chicken is evenly coated.

Spray a large frying pan (skillet) with some low-calorie cooking spray and place over a medium heat. Add the onions and fry for a few minutes until softened, then add the coated chicken and cook for 7 minutes until browned. Add the passata, 50ml (1¾fl oz/3½ tablespoons) water and the crumbled stock cube and remaining spice mix, then reduce the heat and stir through the butter. Mix until it has melted.

Stir through the Greek yoghurt before serving, and sprinkle with coriander.

~~~~

Notes Refrigerate for up to 3 days.

To make this vegetarian, use Quorn instead of chicken.

SPEEDY PREP

SLOW COOK

I know what you're thinking, 'How is a slow cooker speedy?'. Well, the beauty of the slow cooker is that it does much of the hard work for you in advance so that you don't have to.

These recipes are super simple to prepare, so simple in fact, that you can mostly just chuck everything in the slow cooker in the morning before you start your day, and leave it to cook away in the slow cooker while you're busy. Then a delicious home-cooked meal is ready and waiting for you in the evening!

If you don't have a slow cooker, I really recommend getting your hands on one. You can pick them up extremely cheaply, and they remove so much hassle from cooking.

Not only that, but they are actually a much cheaper way to cook as well. While they take longer to cook a meal, they're rated at as little as 200 Watts, which is less than a tenth of some electric ovens.

Also, when you cook meat in a slow cooker over a longer period of time, it softens the connective tissue making it fall apart and become extremely tender.

There is so much more to slow cooking than just stews and casseroles, with a whole host of delicious dinners that you can create.

creamy chicken, tomato and basil spaghetti

Tomato and basil is such a classic flavour combination, and this dish has a future classic written all over it. The creamy sauce is delicious, and the spaghetti can be cooked directly in the slow cooker, saving on washing up.

MAKES 4 PORTIONS

1 x 400g (14oz) tin of
    chopped tomatoes
1 x 500g (1lb 2oz) carton of
    passata (sieved tomatoes)
2 garlic cloves, finely
    diced
1 teaspoon dried basil
4 skinless, boneless chicken
    breasts
2 tablespoons finely chopped
    basil leaves
½ teaspoon smoked paprika
Pinch each of sea salt and
    freshly ground black
    pepper
180g (6oz) dried spaghetti
75g (2¾oz) low-fat cream
    cheese

Prep time 5 minutes | **Cook time** 4 hours on High or 8 hours on Low | **Calorie count** 440 calories per portion

Switch on the slow cooker, then put all the ingredients, except the spaghetti and cream cheese, into the slow cooker. Cover and cook for 4 hours on High or 8 hours on Low.

In the last 30 minutes of cooking time, add the cream cheese and stir until melted. Add the dried spaghetti, replace the lid and cook for the remaining 30 minutes or until the spaghetti is cooked through.

~~~~~

Notes Refrigerate for up to 5 days. Reheat fully to serve.

To cook this dish in the oven, put the ingredients in a large casserole dish (Dutch oven), cover and cook at 180°C/160°C fan/350°F/Gas mark 4 for 2 hours (half the High slow cooker time).

cider and sweet potato casserole

This vegan dish is perfect for meat-free days and is full of comfort. The alcohol cooks off, so no worries about getting drunk on this dish! The cider and the sweetness of the sweet potato make for a delectable mouthful! Serve on its own or with rice.

MAKES 4 PORTIONS

150ml (5fl oz/⅔ cup)
   vegetable stock
2 large sweet potatoes,
   peeled and cut into
   small cubes
1 onion, sliced
1 red (bell) pepper,
   deseeded and sliced
1 yellow (bell) pepper,
   deseeded and sliced
2 garlic cloves, finely
   diced
100g (3½oz) closed-cup
   mushrooms, sliced
1 x 440ml (14¾fl oz) can
   of dry (hard) cider
1 tablespoon cider vinegar
Pinch each of sea salt and
   freshly ground black
   pepper
2 tablespoons vegan coconut
   yoghurt

Prep time 10 minutes | **Cook time** 4 hours on High or 8 hours on Low | **Calorie count** 350 calories per portion

Switch on the slow cooker, then put all the ingredients, except the coconut yoghurt, into the slow cooker. Stir to combine, cover and cook for 4 hours on High or 8 hours on Low.

Just before serving, stir through the coconut yoghurt to add creaminess.

Notes Refrigerate for up to 5 days.
Reheat fully before serving.

To cook this casserole in the oven, put
the ingredients in a large casserole dish
(Dutch oven), cover and cook at 180°C/
160°C fan/350°F/Gas mark 4 for 2 hours
(half the High slow cooker time).

pulled smoked paprika jackfruit

The possibilities with this vegan version of pulled pork are endless, as there are so many ways you can serve it – on a jacket potato, as tacos, or even just in a bun on its own.

MAKES 4 PORTIONS

2 x 410g (14½oz) tins of
    jackfruit in water,
    drained
1 red onion, finely diced
1 garlic clove, finely
    chopped
1 x 500g (1lb 2oz) carton of
    passata (sieved tomatoes)
2 tablespoons smoked paprika
1 tablespoon Worcestershire
    sauce
1 tablespoon balsamic
    vinegar
Large pinch each of sea salt
    and freshly ground black
    pepper

Prep time 5 minutes | **Cook time** 4 hours on High or 8 hours on Low | **Calorie count** 225 calories per portion

Switch on the slow cooker, then put all the ingredients into the slow cooker. Stir to combine, then cover and cook for 4 hours on High or 8 hours on Low.

After the cooking time, use two forks to shred up the jackfruit.

Notes Refrigerate for up to 5 days. Reheat fully to serve.

To cook this dish in the oven, put the ingredients in a large casserole dish (Dutch oven), cover and cook at 180°C/ 160°C fan/350°F/Gas mark 4 for 2 hours (half the High slow cooker time).

curried sweet potato, chickpea and coconut stew

Even the biggest meat fans will love this vegan-friendly stew! When I tested this recipe, I was at home all day and the smell was absolutely amazing. I love this served just with crusty wholemeal bread.

MAKES 4 PORTIONS

2 large sweet potatoes, peeled and diced into small cubes
½ teaspoon ground cinnamon
½ teaspoon ground turmeric
½ teaspoon ground cumin
½ teaspoon ground coriander
¼ teaspoon dried chilli (hot red pepper) flakes
1 yellow onion, sliced
3 garlic cloves, finely diced
1 x 400g (14oz) tin of chopped tomatoes
1 x 400g (14oz) tin of chickpeas (garbanzo beans), drained
100ml (3½fl oz/scant ½ cup) vegetable stock
1 x 400ml (14fl oz) tin of light coconut milk
Pinch each of sea salt and freshly ground black pepper
Juice of 1 lime
70g (2½oz) spinach leaves

Prep time 10 minutes | **Cook time** 4 hours on High or 8 hours on Low | **Calorie count** 495 calories per portion

Put the cubed sweet potato in a bowl with the cinnamon, turmeric, cumin, coriander and chilli flakes and toss until the sweet potato is coated in the spice mixture.

Switch on the slow cooker, then put the sweet potato, plus any excess spices left in the bowl, into the slow cooker. Add the rest of the ingredients (except the spinach), stir to combine, cover and cook for 4 hours on High or 8 hours on Low.

Stir through the spinach just before serving, until it wilts.

Notes Refrigerate for up to 5 days or freeze for up to 3 months. Reheat fully to serve.

To cook this dish in the oven, put the ingredients in a large casserole dish (Dutch oven), cover, and cook at 180°C/160°C fan/350°F/Gas mark 4 for 2 hours (half the High slow cooker time).

coconut, chicken and butter bean casserole

This casserole is a hearty and flavourful dish that combines the richness of coconut milk, the tenderness of chicken, and the creaminess of butter beans. Delicious served on its own or with some bread for dipping.

MAKES 4 PORTIONS

4 skinless, boneless chicken breasts
2 x 400g (14oz) tins of butter beans, drained
1 x 400ml (14fl oz) tin of light coconut milk
2 carrots, peeled and cut into large slices
3 baby shallots, peeled
1 red (bell) pepper, deseeded and thinly sliced
1 yellow (bell) pepper, deseeded and thinly sliced
1 garlic clove, crushed
1 teaspoon sweet paprika
1 leek, sliced into rounds
50ml (1¾fl oz/3½ tablespoons) white wine
2 tablespoons Worcestershire sauce
250ml (8fl oz/1 cup) chicken stock
1 celery stick, thinly sliced
250g (9oz) cherry tomatoes
Pinch each of sea salt and freshly ground black pepper

Prep time 5 minutes | **Cook time** 4 hours on High or 8 hours on Low | **Calorie count** 420 calories per portion

Switch on the slow cooker and put all the ingredients into the slow cooker. Cover and cook for 4 hours on High or 8 hours on Low.

You can leave the chicken breasts whole or shred them with two forks.

~~~~~

Notes Refrigerate for up to 5 days or freeze for up to 3 months. Reheat fully before serving.

To cook this dish in the oven, put the ingredients in a large casserole dish (Dutch oven), cover and cook at 180°C/160°C fan/350°F/Gas mark 4 for 2 hours (half the High slow cooker time).

chicken and chorizo mexican-style rice

A tasty, spicy little rice dish made with brown rice. The chicken is so succulent, and the rice soaks up the warming spices. The ingredients are really good value, making it both budget-friendly and time friendly.

MAKES 4 PORTIONS

500g (1lb 2oz) skinless, boneless chicken thighs, cut into small chunks

110g (3¾oz) sliced chorizo, cut into strips

1 large red onion, finely diced

1 red (bell) pepper, deseeded and sliced

2 garlic cloves, finely diced

1 tablespoon sweet paprika

1 tablespoon ground cumin

½ teaspoon red chilli powder

550ml (18fl oz/2½ cups) chicken stock

Pinch each of sea salt and freshly ground black pepper

200g (7oz) brown rice

Prep time 5 minutes | **Cook time** 4 hours on High or 8 hours on Low | **Calorie count** 500 calories per portion

Switch on the slow cooker then put all the ingredients except the rice into the slow cooker. Cover and cook for 4 hours on High or 8 hours on Low.

For the last hour of cooking, stir in the rice. Replace the lid and cook for the remaining hour, stirring occasionally until the rice has cooked through.

Notes Refrigerate for up to 3 days. Reheat fully before serving.

To cook this dish in the oven, put the ingredients in a large casserole dish (Dutch oven), cover and cook at 180°C/160°C fan/350°F/Gas mark 4 for 2 hours (half the High slow cooker time).

hunter's chicken dinner

An absolute classic meal. This all-in-one way of slow cooking the dish with some potatoes means the whole dinner is ready in one go. Serve with some microwave steamed veg.

MAKES 2 PORTIONS

2 large skinless, boneless chicken breasts

4 rashers of smoked bacon medallions (or normal bacon with the fat removed)

250g (9oz) new potatoes, skin on, halved

80g (2¾oz) extra-light Cheddar cheese, grated

Sea salt and freshly ground black pepper

For the BBQ sauce

1 x 500g (1lb 2oz) carton of passata (sieved tomatoes)

5 tablespoons Worcestershire sauce

3 tablespoons balsamic vinegar

1 teaspoon English mustard powder

2 garlic cloves, crushed

1 teaspoon smoked paprika

3 tablespoons granulated sweetener

120ml (4fl oz/½ cup) Coke Zero

1 beef stock cube, crumbled

Pinch each of sea salt and freshly ground black pepper

Prep time 10 minutes | **Cook time** 4 hours on High or 8 hours on Low | **Calorie count** 570 calories per portion

Combine the sauce ingredients in bowl with a pinch each of salt and pepper, mixing well.

Wrap the chicken breasts in the bacon. Place on a large square of foil, then pull the 4 corners up to enclose the chicken but leave the top of the parcel open. Pour the BBQ sauce into each partially closed parcel.

Turn the slow cooker on. Layer the new potatoes on the base of the slow cooker, sprinkle with salt and pepper, then add your chicken parcels on top.

In the last 30 minutes of cooking, carefully add 40g (1½oz) of cheese into each parcel, then replace the lid and cook for the remaining 30 minutes. Serve once the cheese has melted.

～～～

Notes Leftover BBQ sauce can be kept in the refrigerator for up to 5 days and used as a dipping sauce. The whole dish can be chilled and kept in the refrigerator for up to 3 days, and can be frozen too. Reheat fully before serving.

To cook this dish in the oven, put the ingredients in a large casserole dish (Dutch oven), cover and cook at 180°C/160°C fan/350°F/Gas mark 4 for 2 hours (half the High slow cooker time).

creamy boursin, chorizo and chicken casserole

This is such a tasty, herby chicken casserole. It is perfect when served on its own, or even with some crusty bread dipped into it! The Boursin adds such a yummy creaminess, as well as its herb flavours.

MAKES 4 PORTIONS

1 red onion, finely diced

1 red (bell) pepper, deseeded and finely diced

1 yellow (bell) pepper, deseeded and finely diced

200g (7oz) new potatoes, quartered

100g (3½oz) closed-cup mushrooms, sliced

40g (1½oz) chorizo, cut into slices

500g (1lb 2oz) skinless, boneless chicken breast, diced

1 x 500g (1lb 2oz) carton of passata (sieved tomatoes)

150ml (5fl oz/⅔ cup) chicken stock

Pinch each of sea salt and freshly ground black pepper

1 teaspoon smoked paprika

75g (2¾oz) Boursin cheese, plus a little extra for the top

A few parsley leaves, chopped, to serve

Prep time 5 minutes | **Cook time** 4 hours on High or 8 hours on Low | **Calorie count** 440 calories per portion

Switch on the slow cooker, then put all the ingredients, except the Boursin cheese and parsley, into the slow cooker. Stir to combine, then cover and cook for 4 hours on High or 8 hours on Low.

In the last 30 minutes of cooking time, add the Boursin cheese then replace the lid and cook for the remaining 30 minutes, stirring regularly as the cheese melts.

Serve with a little more Boursin crumbled on top, and garnish with some parsley.

Notes Refrigerate for up to 5 days. Reheat fully to serve.

To cook this dish in the oven, put the ingredients in a large casserole dish (Dutch oven), cover and cook at 180°C/160°C fan/350°F/Gas mark 4 for 2 hours (half the High slow cooker time).

cheesy cowboy hotpot

This cheap and cheerful recipe was an absolute staple when I first left home and money was tight. It can be made up predominantly of tinned vegetables and is easy to adapt to suit any taste. This isn't a traditional hotpot, but it's just what I used to call it at the time, so the name has stuck! It's perfect on its own or with some bread for dipping.

MAKES 4 PORTIONS

1 large potato, peeled and cut into small cubes

6 lean pork sausages, chopped

4 smoked bacon medallions, chopped

1 large onion, sliced

2 x 400g (14oz) tins of baked beans

1 red (bell) pepper, deseeded and sliced

1 x 200g (7oz) tin of sweetcorn, drained

200g (7oz) tinned marrowfat peas, drained

200g (7oz) tinned green beans, drained

1 teaspoon tomato purée (paste)

2 teaspoons smoked paprika

1 tablespoon Worcestershire sauce

1 tablespoon balsamic vinegar

1 beef stock cube, crumbled

Pinch each of sea salt and freshly ground black pepper

160g (5½oz) reduced-fat Cheddar cheese, grated

Prep time 5 minutes | **Cook time** 4 hours on High or 8 hours on Low | **Calorie count** 550 calories per portion

Switch on the slow cooker, then put all the ingredients, except the cheese, into the slow cooker. Stir to combine, cover and cook for 4 hours on High or 8 hours on Low.

In the last 30 minutes of cooking, sprinkle the cheese over the top then replace the lid. Leave to cook for the remaining 30 minutes until the cheese has melted.

~~~~

Notes Can be refrigerated for up to 5 days. Reheat fully before serving.

To cook this dish in the oven, put the ingredients in a large casserole dish (Dutch oven), cover and cook at 180°C/160°C fan/350°F/Gas mark 4 for 2 hours (half the High slow cooker time).

To make this vegetarian, use veggie sausages, leave out the bacon and use a vegetable stock cube.

asian-style BBQ pork loin and root veg

This Asian-inspired pork loin joint is full of sticky sweet flavours. I enjoy it on its own with the root veggies, but it is also delicious served with rice. Any leftover pork can be kept and used in sandwiches the next day. It is so juicy and succulent.

MAKES 4 PORTIONS

700g (1lb 9oz) boneless pork loin joint, excess fat removed

For the sauce

2 teaspoons sea salt

½ teaspoon Chinese five-spice

¼ teaspoon ground white pepper

½ teaspoon toasted sesame oil

1 tablespoon rice vinegar

2 tablespoons dark soy sauce

1 tablespoon hoisin sauce

3 garlic cloves, finely minced

2 tablespoons runny honey

1 tablespoon hot water

For the vegetables

3 carrots, peeled and roughly chopped

2 parsnips, peeled and roughly chopped

2 onions, peeled and roughly chopped

1 large potato, peeled and roughly chopped

Prep time 10 minutes | **Cook time** 4 hours on High or 8 hours on Low | **Calorie count** 521 calories per portion

Mix together the sauce ingredients in a bowl. Score the pork, then rub the sauce all over the joint.

Switch on the slow cooker and add the vegetables. Place the pork loin on top, then cover and cook for 4 hours on High or 8 hours on Low.

Baste the meat twice during the cooking time with any of the sauce that gathers on the bottom.

Notes Refrigerate for up to 5 days. Reheat fully before serving.

To cook this dish in the oven, put the ingredients in a large casserole dish (Dutch oven), cover and cook at 180°C/160°C fan/350°F/Gas mark 4 for 2 hours (half the High slow cooker time).

chilli con carne rice

I love a good chilli, and one that is so simple to prepare is even better! I like to add the rice directly into the chilli to make a perfect one-pot meal. You can adjust the spice levels by adding more or fewer chillies and tweaking how much cayenne pepper you add.

MAKES 4 PORTIONS

1 large red onion, finely diced
2 garlic cloves, crushed and finely chopped
2 red (bell) peppers, deseeded and sliced
2 fresh chillies, deseeded and chopped (adjust the spice to your taste!)
500g (1lb 2oz) extra-lean 5%-fat minced (ground) beef
2 teaspoons ground cumin
1 teaspoon ground coriander
1 teaspoon smoked paprika
Pinch of cayenne pepper
2 x 400g (14oz) tins of chopped tomatoes
300ml (10fl oz/1¼ cups) beef stock
Pinch each of sea salt and freshly ground black pepper
1 x 400g (14oz) tin of red kidney beans
1 beef stock cube, crumbled
220g (7¾oz) pack of microwave long-grain rice, cooked
1 tablespoon reduced-fat sour cream, per portion, to serve

Prep time 5 minutes | **Cook time** 4 hours on High or 8 hours on Low | **Calorie count** 570 calories per portion

Switch on the slow cooker, then put all the ingredients, except the cooked rice and sour cream, into the slow cooker. Stir to combine, then cover and cook for 4 hours on High or 8 hours on Low.

In the last 30 minutes of cooking time, add the cooked rice, replace the lid and continue to cook for the remaining 30 minutes.

Serve with a tablespoon of sour cream on each serving.

Notes Refrigerate for up to 2 days. Reheat fully to serve.

To cook this dish in the oven, put the ingredients in a large casserole dish (Dutch oven), cover and cook at 180°C/160°C fan/350°F/Gas mark 4 for 2 hours (half the High slow cooker time).

To make this dish dairy free, leave out the sour cream.

korean-style beef noodles

This Korean-inspired dish is salty, sweet and super filling. The beef should fall apart as it is slowly cooked. You can add the noodles to the slow cooker as well, so there is no need to use a separate saucepan!

MAKES 4 PORTIONS

750g (1lb 10oz) lean diced beef (can be casserole beef or braising steak cut into chunks)

1 onion, diced

2 garlic cloves, finely diced

2 teaspoons 'lazy' ginger from a jar (or a generous thumb-sized piece of fresh ginger, grated)

1 tablespoon rice vinegar

2 tablespoons toasted sesame oil

60ml (2fl oz/¼ cup) dark soy sauce

60ml (2fl oz/¼ cup) light soy sauce

120ml (4fl oz/½ cup) beef stock (made from a cube) and 1 extra beef stock cube, crumbled

2 tablespoons runny honey

½ teaspoon dried chilli (hot red pepper) flakes

2 x 50g (1¾oz) nests of dried egg noodles

White sesame seeds, to serve

Prep time 5 minutes | **Cook time** 4 hours on High or 8 hours on Low | **Calorie count** 520 calories per portion

Switch on the slow cooker, then put all the ingredients, except the noodles and sesame seeds, into the slow cooker. Stir to combine, then cover and cook for 4 hours on High or 8 hours on Low.

In the last 30 minutes of cooking time, add the noodles, replace the lid and cook for the remaining 30 minutes.

Check the noodles are cooked through and coated in the sauce and serve with some sesame seeds sprinkled on the top.

~~~~

Notes I don't braise the beef in this recipe, but you can if you prefer.

Refrigerate for up to 5 days or freeze for up to 2 months. Reheat fully to serve.

To cook the beef in the oven, put the ingredients in a large casserole dish (Dutch oven), cover and cook at 180°C/160°C fan/350°F/Gas mark 4 for 2 hours (half the High slow cooker time).

beef curry

This delicious, rich beef curry is aromatic and so easy to prepare thanks to it being a slow cooker recipe! The beef will be so tender that it will melt in the mouth and be full of flavour. This is delicious served on its own, with green vegetables, or with rice.

Prep time 5 minutes | **Cook time** 4 hours on High or 8 hours on Low | **Calorie count** 350 calories per portion

MAKES 4 PORTIONS

750g (1lb 10oz) lean diced beef (casserole beef or braising steak cut into chunks)

1 large onion, sliced

2 red (bell) peppers, deseeded and diced

3 garlic cloves, finely diced

1 teaspoon 'lazy' ginger from a jar (or a thumb-sized piece of fresh ginger, grated)

2 tablespoons medium curry powder

2 tablespoons garam masala

1 teaspoon dried chilli flakes

1 beef stock cube, crumbled

1 x 400g (14oz) tin of chopped tomatoes

2 tablespoons tomato purée (paste)

1 x 400ml (14fl oz) tin of light coconut milk

Juice of 1 lime

Pinch each of sea salt and freshly ground black pepper

Handful of coriander (cilantro) leaves

Handful of spinach leaves

Switch on the slow cooker, then put all the ingredients, except the coriander and spinach leaves, into the slow cooker. Stir to combine, then cover and cook for 4 hours on High or 8 hours on Low.

Once cooked, add the coriander and spinach leaves and stir through until the spinach has wilted.

Notes I don't brown the beef in this recipe before adding it to the slow cooker, but you can if you prefer.

Refrigerate for up to 5 days or freeze for up to 2 months. Reheat fully to serve.

To cook this curry in the oven, put the ingredients in a large casserole dish (Dutch oven), cover and cook at 180°C/160°C fan/350°F/Gas mark 4 for 2 hours (half the High slow cooker time).

peppercorn beef hotpot

Beef and peppercorn are one of those amazing flavour combinations. This delicious hotpot has a peppery kick and sliced potato topping, and is packed with veggies. This is perfect as a winter warmer.

MAKES 4 PORTIONS

750g (1lb 10oz) lean diced beef (casserole beef or braising steak cut into chunks)

1 large onion, finely diced

450ml (15fl oz/ scant 2 cups) beef stock

2 tablespoons Worcestershire sauce

1 tablespoon tomato purée (paste)

2 teaspoons English mustard

125g (4¼oz) carrots, peeled and diced

125g (4¼oz) swede, peeled and diced

125g (4¼oz) parsnip, peeled and diced

2 teaspoons freshly ground black pepper (use a peppercorn grinder to crush them)

Pinch of sea salt

1 tablespoon gravy granules

Low-calorie cooking spray

400g (14oz) potatoes, thinly sliced (skin on)

Prep time 10 minutes | **Cook time** 4 hours on High or 8 hours on Low | **Calorie count** 490 calories per portion

Switch on the slow cooker, then put all the ingredients, except the low-calorie cooking spray and sliced potatoes, into the slow cooker. Stir to combine, then layer over the sliced potatoes. Press them down so that the bottom ones sit in the sauce, then spray with low-calorie cooking spray. Cover and cook for 4 hours on High or 8 hours on Low.

Notes If you want crispy potatoes, you could place the dish under a hot grill (broiler) before serving.

I don't brown the beef in this recipe, but you can if you prefer.

Refrigerate for up to 5 days or freeze for up to 2 months. Reheat fully to serve.

To cook this hotpot in the oven, put the ingredients in a large casserole dish (Dutch oven), cover, and cook at 180°C/160°C fan/350°F/Gas mark 4 for 2 hours (half the High slow cooker time).

slow-cooker roast beef dinner

I love cooking a joint of beef in the slow cooker with loads of tasty root vegetables underneath, making a Sunday roast extra easy! The leftover juices can also be made into a yummy gravy.

MAKES 4 PORTIONS

1kg (2lb 4oz) lean rolled beef brisket (any excess fat removed)

1 tablespoon sunflower oil

3 carrots, sliced

3 celery sticks, sliced

2 parsnips, peeled and chopped

1 onion, sliced

2 large potatoes, peeled and chopped

2 garlic cloves, crushed

2 teaspoons English mustard powder

1 teaspoon horseradish sauce from a jar

2 tablespoons red wine vinegar

1 tablespoon balsamic vinegar

350ml (12fl oz/1½ cups) beef stock

Sea salt and freshly ground black pepper

For the gravy

½ tablespoon cornflour (cornstarch)

½ tablespoon cold water

Prep time 15 minutes | **Cook time** 4 hours on High or 8 hours on Low | **Calorie count** 580 calories per portion

Season the beef with a generous amount of salt and pepper.

Heat the oil in a frying pan (skillet) over a high heat, then sear the beef for a few minutes on each side in the hot pan.

Switch on the slow cooker and layer the carrot, celery, parsnip, onion and potatoes on the bottom of the slow cooker. Add the garlic, mustard powder, horseradish, red wine vinegar, balsamic vinegar and stock. Place the beef on top of the vegetables, then pour over the stock. Cover and cook for 4 hours on High or 8 hours on Low.

Remove the beef and either slice it or shred it with two forks.

Remove the vegetables from the slow cooker, leaving any remaining stock and juices in the slow cooker.

Mix the cornflour and water together, then add this to the stock and juices. Stir well to thicken and use for the gravy – if you prefer a thicker gravy, add some more cornflour and water.

Serve the sliced or shredded beef with the veggies and the gravy poured over.

〜〜〜

Notes The beef is delicious in sandwiches the next day if there is any leftover! Refrigerate for up to 3 days.

To cook this dish in the oven, brown the beef first, then put the ingredients in a large casserole dish (Dutch oven), cover and cook at 180°C/160°C fan/350°F/ Gas mark 4 for 2 hours (half the High slow cooker time).

BATCH-COOK

SUNDAY

Batch prepping meals can sometimes seem like a daunting task. While it is easy to think that it could be more effort, it is actually one of my biggest recommendations for time-saving.

I have always loved batch cooking on the weekends to get ahead, and making just a few meals can keep you going all week.

This chapter is a selection of my favourite meals to pre-prepare for the week ahead, so they can either be put straight in the oven to cook or reheated.

A little bit of time investment at the weekend can go a long way towards helping you stay on track during the week. You can also portion control by separating dishes into single servings or keeping them as one to feed a family.

Batch cooking can also help prevent food wastage: I am sure we have all left that vegetable in the refrigerator a little too long because we don't get around to using it. By batch-prepping a week of meals you can buy exactly what you need and use it straight away!

curried cauliflower soup

This zesty, spicy bowl of warmth is perfect for lunches or as a main meal in the evenings. It's so hearty and creamy, and it's great for freezing, too, so you always have some to hand. If you're vegan, make sure the curry paste you use is suitable for your dietary needs by checking the label.

MAKES 5 PORTIONS

1 large cauliflower,
   cut into small chunks
1 large onion, diced
2 garlic cloves,
   finely diced
2 tablespoons Thai red
   curry paste
Grated zest and juice
   of 1 lemon
1 teaspoon white wine
   vinegar
200ml (7fl oz/scant 1 cup)
   light coconut milk
2 teaspoons rice vinegar
350ml (12fl oz/1½ cups)
   vegetable stock
Low-calorie cooking spray
Sea salt and freshly ground
   black pepper

Prep time 5 minutes | **Cook time** 20 minutes |
Calorie count 150 calories per portion

Bring a saucepan of salted water to the boil, add the cauliflower and cook for 7 minutes, or until soft.

Spray a separate large saucepan with some low-calorie cooking spray and place over a medium heat. Add the onion and garlic and fry for 3 minutes, until the onion has softened. Add the curry paste and the zest and juice of the lemon, stir and cook for 1 minute. Add the vinegar, coconut milk, rice vinegar and vegetable stock and stir well. Season with salt and pepper.

Once the cauliflower is cooked, drain and add it to the large saucepan. Reduce the heat and simmer for 5 minutes, then remove from the heat and use a food processor or hand-held blender to blitz the soup until smooth.

Allow to cool, then refrigerate or freeze.

Note Refrigerate for up to 5 days, or pour into freezer bags and freeze for up to 6 months. Defrost and reheat fully before serving.

lasagne soup

This has all the elements of a lasagne, but in a hearty and filling soup instead. I have added my own twist to this social media trend; instead of the béchamel, this soup has the creaminess of ricotta cheese.

MAKES 5 PORTIONS

1 red onion, finely diced
2 garlic cloves, finely diced
500g (1lb 2oz) extra-lean 5%-fat minced (ground) beef
2 tablespoons tomato purée (paste)
1 x 500g (1lb 2oz) carton of passata (sieved tomatoes)
½ teaspoon dried chilli (hot red pepper) flakes
2 teaspoons dried parsley
½ teaspoon dried oregano
1 teaspoon dried basil
200ml (7fl oz/scant 1 cup) beef stock
4 lasagne sheets, broken roughly into quarters
3 tablespoons ricotta cheese
Low-calorie cooking spray
Sea salt and freshly ground black pepper

Prep time 10 minutes | **Cook time** 15 minutes | **Calorie count** 280 calories per portion

Spray a large saucepan with some low-calorie cooking spray and place over a medium heat. Add the onion and garlic and cook for 3 minutes until softened. Add the beef and fry for about 5 minutes until browned, breaking up the mince with a wooden spoon as it cooks.

Stir in the tomato purée, passata, chilli flakes, herbs and stock. Bring to the boil, then add the broken lasagne sheets to the pan. Reduce the heat and cook for about 10 minutes until the lasagne is tender.

To server, add the ricotta cheese, season with salt and pepper and stir.

Notes Refrigerate for up to 5 days, or pour into freezer bags and freeze for up to 6 months. Defrost and reheat fully before serving.

You can add an extra spoonful of ricotta to the bowl when serving the soup, if you like, but just bear in mind that this will affect the calorie count.

spicy butternut squash mac 'n' cheese

A different take on mac 'n' cheese, with a delicious spicy sauce made from butternut squash.

MAKES 4 PORTIONS

½ butternut squash (about 500 g/17½oz), deseeded and cut into small cubes
300g (10½oz) dried macaroni
½ onion, finely chopped
2 garlic cloves, crushed
1 teaspoon cayenne pepper
1 tablespoon sriracha sauce
1 tablespoon English mustard powder
400ml (14fl oz/1¾ cups) vegetable stock
160g (5½oz) reduced-fat Cheddar cheese, grated
30g (1oz) Parmesan, grated
1 tablespoon low-fat cream cheese
Low-calorie cooking spray
Sea salt and freshly ground black pepper

Prep time 10 minutes | **Cook time** 55 minutes | **Calorie count** 595 calories per portion

If cooking ahead of time, preheat the oven to 220°C/200°C fan/425°F/Gas mark 7.

Place the cubed butternut squash on a baking tray (sheet), spray with low-calorie cooking spray, season generously with salt and pepper and bake for about 35 minutes or until softened.

Meanwhile, cook the macaroni in a saucepan of salted boiling water according to the packet instructions.

Spray a large saucepan with some low-calorie cooking spray and place over a medium heat. Add the onion and garlic and fry for a few minutes until softened.

Once the butternut squash is cooked, remove and add it to the saucepan with the garlic and onion. Add the cayenne pepper, sriracha and mustard powder and mix together. Add the stock and bring to the boil, then remove from the heat, transfer to a food processor and blitz until completely smooth (or use a hand-held blender).

Once smooth, return the mixture to the saucepan and add half the Cheddar and all the Parmesan and cream cheese and mix together until melted.

Retain a couple of tablespoons of the pasta cooking water, then drain. Add the pasta to the sauce with the retained pasta cooking water and mix well.

Spoon into an ovenproof dish, top with the remaining Cheddar, cover and refrigerate.

When ready to cook, bake for 20 minutes until hot throughout and the cheese is bubbling.

Notes Prep and refrigerate for up to 5 days, to cook when you're ready to eat, or cook ahead of time, refrigerate and then reheat fully before serving.

To make this gluten free, substitute the pasta for a gluten-free equivalent.

smoky bean burrito bowls

These bowls are brimming with Mexican-inspired flavours, with a smoky taste from the smoked paprika and a little spicy kick. You can prep the burrito filling ahead of time and freeze or refrigerate it, then serve it with some salad, rice and tortilla chips whenever it's needed.

MAKES 5 PORTIONS

1 onion, finely diced

1 garlic clove, finely diced

1 red (bell) pepper, deseeded and finely diced

1 x 400g (14oz) tin of red kidney beans, drained

1 x 400g (14oz) tin of cannellini beans, drained

2 x 400g (14oz) tins of chopped tomatoes

2 teaspoons garlic granules

2 teaspoons red chilli powder

2 teaspoons ground cumin

4 teaspoons smoked paprika

Low-calorie cooking spray

Pinch each of sea salt and black pepper

To serve

220g (7¾oz) pack of microwave long-grain rice, cooked

40g (1½oz) reduced-fat Cheddar cheese, grated, per portion

Shredded lettuce

15g (½oz) tortilla chips per portion

Coriander (cilantro) leaves

Lime wedges

Prep time 5 minutes | **Cook time** 20 minutes | **Calorie count** 520 calories per portion

Spray a frying pan (skillet) with some low-calorie cooking spray and place over a medium heat. Add the onion, garlic and diced pepper and cook for 3 minutes until softened, then add the two tins of drained beans and fry for 5 minutes.

Add the chopped tomatoes, garlic granules, chilli powder, cumin and paprika, and season with the sea salt and black pepper. Lower the heat and simmer for 10 minutes until reduced to a thickened sauce.

Allow to cool, then refrigerate or freeze.

When serving, pile the hot chilli onto the rice and top with the cheese, lettuce, tortilla chips, coriander and lime wedges for squeezing.

Notes Refrigerate for up to 5 days, or pour into freezer bags and freeze for up to 6 months. Defrost and reheat fully before serving.

Make this vegan and gluten free by leaving out the cheese and tortilla chips.

spicy, sticky halloumi with orzo and chickpeas

This light yet filling orzo dish is delicious either hot or cold. I like to make a big batch at the start of the week and eat it for lunch for the rest of the week.

MAKES 4 PORTIONS

200g (7oz) light halloumi
   cheese, cut into small
   chunks
Low-calorie cooking spray

For the glaze

2 tablespoons runny honey
1 teaspoon dried chilli (hot
   red pepper) flakes
½ garlic clove, finely diced

For the orzo

200g (7oz) orzo
1 red onion, sliced
1 garlic clove, grated
1 x 400g (14oz) tin of
   chopped tomatoes
2 teaspoons dried basil
Large pinch each of sea salt
   and black pepper
1 x 400g (14oz) tin of
   chickpeas (garbanzo
   beans), drained

Prep time 5 minutes | **Cook time** 15 minutes | **Calorie count** 490 calories per portion

Mix the glaze ingredients together in a dish and add the halloumi chunks.

Spray a frying pan (skillet) with some low-calorie cooking spray and place over a medium heat. Add the coated halloumi chunks and cook for 5 minutes until sticky, then remove and set aside. Keep any leftover glaze for later.

Meanwhile, cook the orzo in salted boiling water according to the packet instructions.

Spray some more low-calorie cooking spray in the same pan you used for the halloumi. Place over a medium heat, add the onion and garlic and fry for 2 minutes until softened. Add the chopped tomatoes, basil, salt, pepper and drained chickpeas, and cook for 5 minutes over a low heat.

Once the orzo is cooked, add it to the pan of tomato and chickpeas and mix well, then add in the cooked halloumi and any excess glaze and stir to combine.

Note Refrigerate for up to 5 days in a sealed container. Reheat fully before serving.

meat-free moussaka

This vegan version of the well-known Middle Eastern dish uses soya mince instead of lamb. It's perfect to portion up so you have dinner ready for the week.

MAKES 4 PORTIONS

160g (5½oz) soya mince
2 aubergines (eggplants), cut into medium slices
1 onion, finely chopped
2 garlic cloves, crushed
3 teaspoons dried oregano
1 teaspoon ground cinnamon
1 x 400g (14oz) tin of chopped tomatoes
2 tablespoons tomato purée (paste)
200g (7oz) Maris Piper potatoes, peeled and thinly sliced
Low-calorie cooking spray
Sea salt and freshly ground black pepper

For the white sauce

40g (1½oz/¼ cup) plain (all-purpose) flour
400ml (14fl oz/1⅔ cups) unsweetened almond milk
2 tablespoons nutritional yeast flakes
1 bay leaf
¼ teaspoon ground nutmeg
80g (2¾oz) vegan mozzarella-style cheese

Note Prep and refrigerate for up to 5 days, to cook when you're ready to eat, or cook ahead of time and reheat fully before serving.

Prep time 15 minutes | **Cook time** 1 hour 15 minutes | **Calorie count** 420 calories per portion

If cooking ahead of time, preheat the oven to 220°C/200°C fan/ 425°F/Gas mark 7.

Put the soya mince in a heatproof bowl with 600ml (20fl oz/ 2½ cups) boiling water. Stir and leave to stand for 5 minutes.

Meanwhile, spray a frying pan (skillet) with some low-calorie cooking spray and place over a medium heat. Add the sliced aubergine (eggplant) and fry for 5–7 minutes, turning over to brown both sides, until golden brown and beginning to soften. Remove and set aside on some paper towels.

Spray the pan with more low-calorie cooking spray, add the rehydrated soya mince and cook over a medium heat for 5–10 minutes until browned. Once browned, set aside.

Add the onion and a pinch of salt to the pan and fry gently for 2 minutes until softened, then add the garlic, oregano and cinnamon and cook for a further minute. Return the soya mince to the pan and stir through the tomatoes and tomato purée along with 200ml (7fl oz/scant 1 cup) water. Season with salt and pepper, reduce the heat and simmer gently, uncovered, for 5 minutes, stirring occasionally, until the sauce has thickened.

Parboil the potato slices in a saucepan of salted boiling water for about 4 minutes, then drain and set aside.

Meanwhile, prepare the white sauce. Put the flour, almond milk, yeast flakes, bay leaf and nutmeg in a saucepan and season with salt and pepper. Bring the sauce to a low simmer, whisking constantly, and cook for 4–5 minutes until smooth and thickened. Stir in the cheese and cook for 1–2 minutes more.

Spoon a third of the mince mixture into a large ovenproof dish, then add a layer of aubergine and potato. Repeat and finish off with the white sauce. Refrigerate until ready to cook, or cook straight away in the centre of the oven for 40 minutes.

italian-style veggie and halloumi pesto bake

I love the combination of flavours in this dish, with Mediterranean-style veggies, the 'squeaky cheese' halloumi and pesto giving it an extra edge! It's delicious served on its own as a light, summery dinner, or made heartier with some crusty bread on the side.

MAKES 4 PORTIONS

250g (9oz) light halloumi cheese, cut into 1.5cm (½ inch)-thick slices

3 tablespoons reduced-fat pesto

2 red onions, diced

1 courgette (zucchini), chopped

2 red (bell) peppers, deseeded and sliced

1 yellow (bell) pepper, deseeded and sliced

150g (5½oz) cherry tomatoes, halved

5 pitted olives, sliced

Prep time 5 minutes | **Cook time** 25 minutes | **Calorie count** 320 calories per portion

If cooking ahead of time, preheat the oven to 180°C/160°C fan/350°F/Gas mark 4.

Put the sliced halloumi in a bowl, add 1 tablespoon of the pesto and mix until the halloumi is fully coated.

Lay the prepared vegetables and olives out in an ovenproof dish, then add the remaining 2 tablespoons of pesto. Mix well so that the vegetables are coated in the pesto. Lay the halloumi slices on top of the vegetables.

Either cover and refrigerate until ready to cook, or roast for 25 minutes until the vegetables are cooked and the halloumi is golden.

Note Prep and refrigerate for up to 5 days, to cook when you're ready to eat, or cook ahead of time and reheat fully before serving.

sweet chilli chicken noodles

I make this recipe week in and week out, and have even made it for a selection of Exeter City players while doing meal preps for them. It's quick to rustle up and tastes delicious when reheated.

MAKES 4 PORTIONS

1kg (2lb 4oz) skinless, boneless chicken breasts, diced

640g (1lb 6oz) pre-packed stir-fry vegetables (or a mixture of sliced (bell) peppers, cabbage, carrot and onions)

600g (1lb 5oz) fresh egg noodles

Low-calorie cooking spray

For the sweet chilli sauce

2 garlic cloves, finely grated

2 fresh red chillies, deseeded and finely chopped

160ml (5½fl oz/⅔ cup) white wine vinegar

1 teaspoon sea salt

2 teaspoons granulated sweetener

2 teaspoons tomato purée (paste)

1 tablespoon honey

Prep time 10 minutes | **Cook time** 15 minutes | **Calorie count** 523 calories per portion

Spray a frying pan (skillet) with some low-calorie cooking spray and place over a medium heat, then add the diced chicken. Fry for 7 minutes, or until cooked through, then remove and set aside.

To make the sauce, spray the frying pan (the same one you cooked the chicken in) with low-calorie cooking spray and place over a medium heat. Add the garlic and chilli and fry for about 3 minutes, until softened, then add the white wine vinegar, salt, sweetener and tomato purée, and stir well. Bring to the boil then reduce the heat and cook for 2 minutes. Add the honey and stir well, cooking until the sauce starts to reduce.

Add the vegetables to the sauce and cook for 2 minutes, then add the cooked chicken and the fresh egg noodles. Stir to combine and coat the noodles with the sauce.

If not eating it straight away, allow to cool, then portion and refrigerate until needed.

Note Refrigerate for up to 5 days. Reheat fully before serving.

honey, lemon and garlic chicken thighs

The beauty of this chicken dish is that it pairs well with a range of different side dishes, such as pasta, potatoes or rice. This means you can have a bit of variety throughout the week.

MAKES 4 PORTIONS

8 skinless, boneless
   chicken thighs
1 yellow (bell) pepper,
   deseeded and sliced
1 onion, sliced
Low-calorie cooking spray

For the sauce

2 teaspoons garlic granules
Grated zest of ½ lemon and
   juice of 1 large lemon
3 garlic cloves, finely
   chopped
4 tablespoons honey
Large pinch each of sea salt
   and freshly ground black
   pepper

Prep time 15 minutes | **Cook time** 35 minutes |
Calorie count 270 calories per portion

If cooking ahead of time, preheat the oven to 200°C/180°C fan/400°F/Gas mark 6.

Spray a frying pan (skillet) with some low-calorie cooking spray and place over a medium heat. Add the chicken thighs and cook for 4 minutes on each side until browned.

Mix all of the sauce ingredients together in a bowl.

Put the pepper and onion in a large baking dish. Place the cooked chicken thighs on top, then pour the sauce over the chicken. Allow to cool, then cover and refrigerate, ready to finish cooking during the week, or bake in the oven for 30 minutes, basting the chicken with the sauce halfway through.

~~~

Note Prep and refrigerate for up to 5 days, to cook when you're ready to eat, or cook ahead of time and reheat fully before serving.

mustardy chicken and bacon hot pot

Mustard and bacon is a flavour combination that I absolutely love – no bacon sandwich is complete without mustard! The bacon, chicken and mustard flavours in the dish are so perfect and well balanced, you'll love reheating it for a super quick mid-week meal.

MAKES 4 PORTIONS

3 large potatoes, peeled and thinly sliced, for the topping
1 red onion, finely diced
1 garlic clove, finely chopped
8 smoked bacon medallions, fat removed, meat cut into strips
4 skinless, boneless chicken breasts, diced
2 tablespoons English mustard powder
1 teaspoon wholegrain mustard
½ teaspoon smoked paprika
300ml (10fl oz/1¼ cups) chicken stock
3 tablespoons low-fat cream cheese (or quark)
Low-calorie cooking spray
Sea salt and freshly ground black pepper

Prep time 15 minutes | **Cook time** 55 minutes | **Calorie count** 470 calories per portion

Parboil the potato slices in salted boiling water for 10 minutes, then drain and set aside.

If cooking ahead of time, preheat the oven to 180°C/160°C fan/350°F/Gas mark 4.

Spray a cast-iron casserole dish (or frying pan/skillet if you don't have one) with some low-calorie cooking spray and place over a medium heat. Add the onion and garlic and fry for 3 minutes until softened, then add the bacon and fry for 5 minutes. Add the diced chicken, then the mustard powder, wholegrain mustard and paprika and cook for 7 minutes, until the chicken is cooked through. Add the stock, reduce the heat and simmer for 5 minutes. Stir through the cream cheese, and season with salt and pepper. If you're not using a casserole dish, transfer the mixture to an ovenproof dish.

Lay the parboiled sliced potatoes over the chicken and bacon mixture, then cover and allow to cool before refrigerating until ready to cook.

When ready to cook, bake (uncovered) for 25 minutes until the potatoes are golden.

Note Prep and refrigerate for up to 5 days, to cook when you're ready to eat, or cook ahead of time and reheat fully before serving.

white turkey chilli

You've heard of a chilli con carne, but have you heard of a white chilli? It is essentially the same, but without a tomato base, and involves switching kidney beans for cannellini beans. It's delicious served with rice or tortilla chips.

MAKES 4 PORTIONS

2 onions, diced

2 garlic cloves, diced

500g (1lb 2oz) extra-lean 5%-fat minced (ground) turkey

2 x 400g (14oz) tins of cannellini beans, drained

3 teaspoons red chilli powder (or to taste)

1 teaspoon sweet paprika

1 teaspoon garlic granules

½ teaspoon ground cumin

Large pinch each of sea salt and freshly ground black pepper

Juice of 2 limes

650ml (22fl oz/2¾ cups) chicken stock

250g (9oz) low-fat cream cheese

Low-calorie cooking spray

60g (2¼oz) sliced pickled jalapeños, to serve

Prep time 10 minutes | **Cook time** 20 minutes | **Calorie count** 490 calories per portion

Spray a large saucepan or casserole dish with some low-calorie cooking spray and place over a medium heat. Add the onions and garlic and fry for 3 minutes until softened, then add the turkey and fry for 5 minutes until browned, breaking up the mince with a wooden spoon as it cooks. Add the cannellini beans, chilli powder, paprika, garlic granules and cumin, and the salt and pepper, and stir well. Squeeze in the juice from the limes, then add the stock and reduce the heat to low. Cover the pan and simmer for 10 minutes.

Stir through the cream cheese until it has melted, portion up and finish with the pickled jalapeños just before serving.

Note Refrigerate for up to 5 days, or pour into freezer bags and freeze for up to 6 months. Defrost and reheat fully before serving.

BBQ sausage and pepper pie

These sausages in a yummy BBQ sauce topped with cheesy mashed potato are absolutely incredible. The only issue with this pie will be managing to save it for the week ahead once you have tasted it!

MAKES 4 PORTIONS

2 red onions, sliced

1 red (bell) pepper, deseeded and sliced

1 yellow (bell) pepper, deseeded and sliced

1 green (bell) pepper, deseeded and sliced

1 garlic clove, finely diced

8 lean pork sausages, thickly sliced (chicken sausages also work well)

1 x quantity BBQ Sauce (see page 110)

Low-calorie cooking spray

For the mash topping

500g (1lb 2oz) large potatoes, peeled and cut into small chunks

160g (5½oz) extra-light Cheddar cheese, grated

Prep time 15 minutes | **Cook time** 50 minutes | **Calorie count** 550 calories per portion

If cooking ahead of time, preheat the oven to 200°C/180°C fan/400°F/Gas mark 6.

Spray a frying pan (skillet) with some low-calorie cooking spray and place over a medium heat. Add the onions, peppers and garlic and fry for 4 minutes. Add the sausages to the peppers and onions and fry for 10 minutes, until they are fully cooked.

Meanwhile, cook the potatoes in a saucepan of salted boiling water until they are soft all the way through.

Pour the BBQ sauce over the sausages and peppers. Stir and heat through for 5 minutes, then transfer to a large baking dish.

Mash the potatoes, then use a whisk to beat them briefly and make them extra creamy. Spread the mash over the sausage mixture and top with the grated cheese.

Allow to cool, then cover and refrigerate, ready to finish cooking during the week, or cook ahead of time for 30 minutes, until the pie is bubbling and the cheese has melted.

Notes Prep and refrigerate for up to 5 days, to cook when you're ready to eat, or cook ahead of time and reheat fully before serving. You can also portion and freeze this dish for up to 6 months. Defrost and reheat fully before serving.

creamy cajun bacon tagliatelle

This pasta dish is a twist on a classic recipe from my blog: Creamy Cajun Pasta. The creaminess of the sauce and the smokiness of the bacon, teamed with the Cajun spice, makes this dish so comforting.

MAKES 4 PORTIONS

1 red onion, finely diced

2 garlic cloves, finely diced

1 red (bell) pepper, deseeded and finely diced

1 yellow (bell) pepper, deseeded and finely diced

½ fresh red chilli, finely diced (leave out if you don't want spice!)

100g (3½oz) smoked bacon medallions, fat removed and meat sliced

2 tablespoons Cajun seasoning

410g (14½oz) dried tagliatelle

1 x 180g (6oz) pack of low-fat cream cheese

4 tablespoons tomato purée (paste) or passata (sieved tomatoes)

50ml (1¾fl oz) chicken stock

Low-calorie cooking spray

Sea salt and freshly ground black pepper

Prep time 10 minutes | **Cook time** 15 minutes | **Calorie count** 340 calories per portion

Spray a frying pan (skillet) with some low-calorie cooking spray and place over a medium heat. Add the onion and garlic and fry for 2 minutes until softened. Add the peppers and chilli and fry for a further 2 minutes, then add the sliced bacon and cook for 3 minutes. Add the Cajun seasoning and season with salt and pepper.

Cook the tagliatelle in a saucepan of salted boiling water according to the packet instructions. Retain a few tablespoons of the cooking water once cooked, then drain.

Add the cream cheese, tomato purée (or passata) and chicken stock to the frying pan and stir until the cheese has melted. Add the cooked tagliatelle and the retained pasta cooking water and stir until combined.

Notes Refrigerate for up to 5 days. Reheat fully before serving.

To make this vegetarian, leave out the bacon and switch the chicken stock to vegetable stock.

spicy sausage casserole and dumplings

A hearty sausage casserole with a kick, and yummy lower-fat dumplings. This is the perfect winter comfort food.

MAKES 4 PORTIONS

3 carrots, thinly sliced

50g (1¾oz) button mushrooms, sliced

1 red (bell) pepper, deseeded and sliced

1 yellow (bell) pepper, deseeded and sliced

1 red onion, sliced

8 lean pork sausages, about 50g (1¾oz each) (or lean chicken sausages)

1 large potato, peeled and chopped into small cubes

2 x 500g (17½oz) cartons of passata (sieved tomatoes) and a dash of water

1 teaspoon smoked paprika

Small handful of basil leaves

1 teaspoon dried sage

2 teaspoons dried chilli (hot red pepper) flakes

½ teaspoon red chilli powder

1 garlic clove, finely chopped

1 vegetable stock cube, crumbled

1 x 400g (14oz) tin of low-sugar, low-salt baked beans

1 x 400g (14oz) tin of kidney beans, drained

Low-calorie cooking spray

Sea salt and freshly ground black pepper

For the dumplings

5 tablespoons fat-free Greek yoghurt

6 tablespoons self-raising (self-rising) flour

½ teaspoon baking powder

½ teaspoon dried basil

½ teaspoon dried oregano

Prep time 15 minutes | **Cook time** 1 hour |
Calorie count 550 calories per portion

If cooking ahead of time, preheat the oven to 180°C/160°C fan/350°F/Gas mark 4.

Spray a frying pan (skillet) with some low-calorie cooking spray and place over a medium heat. Add the carrots, mushrooms, peppers and onion and fry for 3 minutes until softened. Remove from the pan and set aside, then add the sausages to the pan and brown them for 5 minutes. Put all of the ingredients for the casserole into a casserole dish, along with the sausages, cover and bake in the oven for 40 minutes.

Meanwhile, make the dumpling mixture by combining all the ingredients in a bowl. You may need to add more flour or yoghurt to make a dough-like consistency. Keep stirring until it forms.

Roll the dumpling mixture into 8 balls, then add to the casserole and press them down into the mixture and cook, uncovered, for a further 20 minutes until the dumplings have risen and are cooked through.

~~~

Notes Prep the casserole (before adding the dumplings) and refrigerate for up to 5 days, to cook when you're ready to eat, or cook ahead of time and reheat fully before serving.

To make this vegetarian, use veggie sausages.

spicy lamb and feta filo pie

Filo (phyllo) pastry is one of my favourite ways to top a pie – it comes out so crispy and delicious. This spicy lamb and feta pie is so summery and light, and is perfect to serve on its own or with some salad.

MAKES 4 PORTIONS

2 red onions, diced

3 garlic cloves, finely chopped

1 red (bell) pepper, deseeded and diced

1 teaspoon 'lazy' ginger from a jar (or a thumb-sized piece of fresh ginger, grated)

1 fresh red chilli, deseeded and finely diced

450g (1lb) extra-lean minced (ground) lamb

6 tablespoons tomato purée (paste)

1 beef stock cube, crumbled

1 tablespoon balsamic vinegar

½ teaspoon ground turmeric

1 teaspoon smoked paprika

100g (3½oz) reduced-fat feta cheese, cut into small cubes

100g (3½oz) filo (phyllo) pastry sheets

Low-calorie cooking spray

Sea salt and freshly ground black pepper

Prep time 15 minutes | **Cook time** 55 minutes | **Calorie count** 450 calories per portion

If cooking ahead of time, preheat the oven to 180°C/160°C fan/350°F/Gas mark 4.

Spray a frying pan (skillet) with some low-calorie cooking spray and place over a medium heat. Add the onion and garlic and cook for 2 minutes until softened, then add the pepper, ginger and chilli and fry for 2 minutes. Add the lamb and cook for 5 minutes until browned, using a wooden spoon to break up the mince, then add the tomato purée, crumbled stock cube, balsamic vinegar, turmeric and smoked paprika. Mix well and season with a large pinch each of salt and pepper. Add the cubed feta and stir to combine.

Put the lamb and feta mixture in an ovenproof dish and bake in the oven for 25 minutes. The dish can be cooled, refrigerated and stored at this stage, until ready to cook with the pastry top, or baked straight away with the filo pastry topping.

When ready to cook, crumple up the filo pastry sheets and place them on top of the pie mixture. This doesn't need to be exact, but make sure that the pie filling is fully covered.

Spray the filo with low-calorie cooking spray and bake in the oven for 20 minutes, until the filling is cooked through and the filo is golden and crisp.

Note Prep (without the filo pastry topping) and refrigerate for up to 5 days, then reheat with the pastry top.

FREEZER BAG

FAVOURITES

I first discovered the beauty of freezer-bag meals when I challenged myself to create 31 dishes that you could prepare in one batch in an hour for a blog post. It went absolutely viral with so many people trying it as well.

Batch prepping and freezer-bag meals go hand in hand, both saving you time and money. The way I look at it is that batch prepping is for the week ahead, yet freezer-meal prepping is for the longer term.

This chapter is for meals that are either 'dump meals', meaning you can put everything in the freezer bag and then straight into the slow cooker, pan or oven on the day you want to prepare it, or are perfect to portion up and freeze so you have them in the freezer for the weeks where you may not have time to prep ahead at the weekend.

If you use freezer bags to store your pre-prepared meals, they take up very little space in the freezer. You can remove all the air from the bag and store them flat.

Preparing freezer-bag meals not only saves you time cooking during the week, but it saves time on planning what you're going to eat each evening. Especially if you have a full freezer at your disposal!

greek-style lemon and chickpea soup

This soup can be prepped ahead of time and left to cook in the slow cooker all day, or heated on the stovetop. The perfect Mediterranean flavours and comfort food combine to make this an absolute staple to have in your freezer.

MAKES 4 PORTIONS

1 large red onion, diced
2 garlic cloves, diced
2 celery sticks, thinly
   sliced
1 carrot, diced
1 teaspoon dried rosemary
2 tablespoons dried oregano
2 x 400g (14oz) tins of
   chickpeas (garbanzo
   beans), drained and
   rinsed
750ml (25fl oz/3 cups)
   vegetable stock
Juice of 2 lemons

Prep time 5 minutes | **Cook time** variable (see method) | **Calorie count** 350 calories per portion

Put all of the ingredients in a large, heavy-duty freezer bag, remove as much air as possible, tightly seal and freeze.

The day before cooking, remove the bag from the freezer and allow the contents to thaw in the refrigerator for 24 hours.

Add to a slow cooker and cook for 4 hours on High, or cook in a large saucepan on the hob over a medium heat for 30 minutes, until the chickpeas have softened.

Notes Add some cooked shredded chicken to the soup if you want some meat.

Once frozen, the soup will keep for up to 3 months.

tomato, chilli and red lentil soup

This hearty, chunky soup is so comforting and has its own little spicy kick. It's perfect to cook from frozen too, so there is no reason not to have a supply of it in your freezer.

MAKES 4 PORTIONS

75g (2¾oz) dried red
   lentils, rinsed in a
   sieve until the water
   runs clear
500ml (17fl oz/? cups)
   cooled vegetable stock
1 red onion, finely diced
1 red chilli, deseeded and
   diced
2 red (bell) peppers,
   deseeded and diced
2 garlic cloves, diced
2 x 400g (14oz) tins of
   chopped tomatoes
1 teaspoon dried basil
Low-calorie cooking spray
Sea salt and freshly ground
   black pepper

Prep time 10 minutes | **Cook time** 10 minutes |
Calorie count 200 calories per portion

Put the lentils in the stock and allow to soak for 10 minutes while you prep the rest of the ingredients.

Spray a frying pan (skillet) with some low-calorie cooking spray and place over a medium heat. Add the onion, chilli, peppers and garlic and fry for 2–3 minutes, then add the tomatoes and basil and season well with salt and pepper.

If you prefer a smoother soup, you can blitz it at this stage with a hand-held blender, but I enjoy it quite chunky.

Drain any remaining stock from the lentils and add the lentils to the soup. Allow to cool, then add to a large, heavy-duty freezer bag, remove as much air as possible, tightly seal and freeze.

Reheat fully from frozen in a saucepan when ready to eat.

Note This soup can be enjoyed chunky
or smooth.

Once frozen, the soup will keep for
up to 3 months.

butter bean and squash curry

This creamy, nutty, spicy curry is a freezer bag 'dump meal', which means you can chuck all of the ingredients into a bag, freeze it, then just defrost overnight and cook in the slow cooker, or in the oven when you're ready!

Prep time 5 minutes | **Cook time** variable – see method | **Calorie count** 430 calories per portion

MAKES 4 PORTIONS

2 x 400g (14oz) tins of butter beans, drained and rinsed

1 large butternut squash, deseeded, peeled and cut into small cubes

1 red (bell) pepper, deseeded cut into small cubes

1 red onion, thinly sliced

2 x 400ml (14fl oz) tins of light coconut milk

1 tablespoon smooth peanut butter

Juice of 1 lime

1 tablespoon tomato purée (paste)

1½ tablespoons curry powder

½ teaspoon garlic granules

½ teaspoon ground ginger

Pinch each of sea salt and freshly ground black pepper

Put the butter beans, butternut squash, pepper and red onion in a large, heavy-duty freezer bag.

Whisk together the coconut milk, peanut butter, lime juice, tomato purée, curry powder, garlic granules, ginger and salt and pepper. Pour this over the rest of the ingredients in the freezer bag, remove as much air as possible, tightly seal and freeze.

The day before cooking, remove the bag from the freezer and allow the contents to thaw in the refrigerator for 24 hours.

Empty the contents of the freezer bag into the slow cooker. Cook on High for 4 hours or low for 7. Alternatively, add to a large casserole dish with a lid and cook in the oven at 180°C/160°C fan/350°F/Gas mark 4 for 1 hour, or until the squash is soft.

Note Once frozen, the curry will keep for up to 3 months.

creamy halloumi, lentil and coconut stew

This vegetarian stew is so warm and tasty. The halloumi has the perfect amount of bite and soaks up all the lovely flavours of the stew when it is cooked. Perfect to prepare and freeze, then defrost and pop straight in the slow cooker or oven when ready to eat.

MAKES 4 PORTIONS

240g (8½oz) block of
   reduced-fat halloumi
   cheese, cut into 2cm
   (¾ inch) cubes
1 onion, diced
1 red (bell) pepper,
   deseeded and thinly
   sliced
1 yellow (bell) pepper,
   deseeded and thinly
   sliced
1 leek, thinly sliced
2 garlic cloves, finely
   diced
1 carrot, diced
1 teaspoon dried parsley
75g (2¾oz) ready-to-eat puy
   lentils
1 x 400g (14oz) tin of
   chopped tomatoes
1 x 400ml (14fl oz) tin of
   light coconut milk
1 x 400g (14oz) tin of
   chickpeas (garbanzo
   beans), drained
Low-calorie cooking spray
Sea salt and freshly ground
   black pepper

Prep time 10 minutes | **Cook time** variable – see method | **Calorie count** 430 calories per portion

Spray a large frying pan (skillet) with some low-calorie cooking spray and place over a medium heat. Add the halloumi and fry for 3 minutes until it starts to go golden, then add the diced onion, peppers, leek, garlic and carrot and fry for 2 minutes. Add the parsley and season with salt and pepper. Add the lentils, tomatoes, coconut milk and chickpeas to the pan, reduce the heat and simmer for 5 minutes.

Allow to cool, then transfer to a large, heavy-duty freezer bag. Remove as much air as possible, tightly seal and freeze.

The day before cooking, remove the bag from the freezer and allow the contents to thaw in the refrigerator for 24 hours.

Cook in a slow cooker on High for 4 hours, or bake in the oven in a casserole dish at 200°C/180°C fan/400°F/Gas mark 6 for 30 minutes until cooked through and bubbling.

Note Once frozen, the stew will keep for up to 3 months.

spinach and ricotta stuffed pasta shells

This meal can be prepped ahead and put straight into the oven when you are ready to eat. I love the creamy spinach filling in these shells, and it is a dish I make over and over again because it's so simple.

MAKES 4 PORTIONS

350g (12½oz) dried conchiglioni (large pasta shells)

250g (9oz) ricotta cheese

3 tablespoons low-fat cream cheese

1 teaspoon dried basil

1 teaspoon dried oregano

1 teaspoon garlic granules

Large pinch each of sea salt and freshly ground black pepper

100g (3½oz) baby spinach leaves

1 x 500g (1lb 2oz) carton of passata (sieved tomatoes)

160g (5½oz) reduced-fat grated mozzarella

Prep time 10 minutes | **Cook time** 30 minutes | **Calorie count** 505 calories per portion

Cook the pasta in a saucepan of salted boiling water for 6 minutes, or until softened but not fully cooked (just before it is al dente).

Combine the ricotta, cream cheese, basil, oregano, garlic granules, salt, pepper and spinach in a bowl.

Put the cheese mixture in a heavy-duty freezer bag, then cut off a corner of the bag so the filling mixture can be squeezed into the shells.

Add half of the passata to the base of a disposable foil tray (or a dish suitable for freezing). Pipe the ricotta mixture into each par-cooked shell, then place them into the tray. Repeat until all the pasta shells are filled, then cover with the rest of the passata. Sprinkle the mozzarella over the top, then wrap the dish in cling film (plastic wrap) and freeze.

The day before cooking, remove the tray from the freezer and allow the contents to thaw in the refrigerator for 24 hours.

When ready to cook, preheat the oven to 200°C/180°C fan/400°F/Gas mark 6. Unwrap the dish and bake for 30 minutes, until the cheese is bubbling.

Notes I like to prepare this dish in a disposable foil tray about 25cm (10 inches) in length, but any dish you are happy to freeze it in will do.

Once frozen, the pasta dish will keep for up to 3 months.

parmesan-crusted cod and lemony new potatoes

This freezer-bag meal can be cooked ahead of time and kept in the freezer, with some lemony new potatoes that you roast in the oven when ready to eat. You just need to reheat the fish fully when ready to serve.

MAKES 4 PORTIONS

For the fish

4 slices of wholemeal bread

85g (3oz) grated Parmesan

½ teaspoon garlic granules

Pinch of sea salt

½ teaspoon smoked paprika

½ teaspoon dried parsley

2 medium eggs

500g (1lb 2oz) skinless, boneless cod, cut into 4 portions

Low-calorie cooking spray

For the potatoes

200g (7oz) new potatoes

Juice of 1 lemon

A few slices of lemon

Prep time 5 minutes | **Cook time** 15 minutes | **Calorie count** 420 calories per portion

Preheat the oven to 200°C/180°C fan/400°F/Gas mark 6, line a baking tray (sheet) with foil and spray it with low-calorie cooking spray.

Par-cook the potatoes in a saucepan of salted boiling water for 7 minutes. Drain, then allow to cool before transferring to a large, heavy-duty freezer bag. Drizzle the potatoes with the lemon juice and add the lemon slices.

Blitz the bread in a food processor to make breadcrumbs. Tip the breadcrumbs into a shallow bowl and mix with the Parmesan, garlic granules, salt, paprika and parsley.

Crack the eggs into a separate shallow bowl and beat them with a fork.

Set up an assembly line from left to right with the fish, eggs, breadcrumb mixture and the baking tray. Dip the fish portions into the egg mixture and then the breadcrumbs, repeating twice to coat fully. Lay each piece of breaded cod onto the lined tray and spray with low-calorie cooking spray.

Bake in the oven for 15 minutes, or until the fish is cooked through and the coating is golden brown and crispy.

Allow to cool, then place the cooked fish in a heavy-duty freezer bag in a single layer. Allow the fish and potatoes to defrost fully before reheating for about 15 minutes at 200°C/180°C fan/ 400°F/Gas mark 6. When cooking the potatoes, put them in an ovenproof dish, spray them with low-calorie cooking spray and roast for 15 minutes.

Note Once frozen, the fish will keep for up to 3 months.

orange and ginger salmon fillets

This has to be one of the quickest meal prep freezer bags to make, as you can put everything in the bag, seal and have it in the freezer within 10 minutes. It's zesty, delicious and perfect for weeknights. Serve with rice or potatoes.

MAKES 4 PORTIONS

500g (1lb 2oz) skinless,
 boneless salmon fillets
1 tablespoon toasted sesame
 oil
1 tablespoon light soy sauce
1 teaspoon ground ginger
Juice of 1 orange
A few slices of orange
2 red onions, cut into
 wedges
100g (3½oz) cherry tomatoes
1 head of broccoli, cut into
 small florets
Sea salt and freshly ground
 black pepper

Prep time 10 minutes | **Cook time** 15 minutes |
Calorie count 400 calories per portion

Put the salmon fillets in a large, heavy-duty freezer bag with the oil, soy sauce, ginger, orange juice, orange slices and a pinch each of salt and pepper. Add the onions, tomatoes and broccoli to the bag. Remove as much air as possible, then tightly seal and freeze.

The day before cooking, remove the bag from the freezer and allow the contents to thaw in the refrigerator for 24 hours.

When ready to cook, preheat the oven to 200°C/180°C fan/400°F/Gas mark 6.

Bake in an ovenproof dish in the oven for 15 minutes, or until the salmon is no longer pink in the middle.

Note Once frozen, the fish will keep for up to 3 months.

crunchy honey BBQ chicken strips

I love making my own chicken strips, but the flavours on these take a regular strip to the next level! They are easy to prepare, crispy and full of flavour. Perfect for popping in the air fryer straight from frozen (or baking in the oven).

Prep time 10 minutes | **Cook time** variable - see method | **Calorie count** 220 calories per portion

MAKES 3 PORTIONS

80g (2¾oz) bran flakes
   or cornflakes
1 medium egg
2 large skinless, boneless
   chicken breasts, cut into
   strips
Low-calorie cooking spray

For the glaze
2 tablespoons runny honey
2 teaspoons smoked paprika
1 garlic clove, finely diced
½ tablespoon dark soy sauce

Put the bran flakes or cornflakes in a freezer bag and use a rolling pin to break them up and form the breadcrumbs.

Crack and whisk the egg in a bowl and dip the chicken strips in, then add them to the bag and shake to coat with the flakes.

Arrange the chicken strips on a baking tray (sheet).

Whisk the glaze ingredients together in a bowl and pour over the top of the chicken strips. Freeze until hard (1–2 hours), then transfer them to a freezer bag and return to the freezer.

When ready to cook, spray the air-fryer basket with low-calorie cooking spray, add the chicken to the air fryer and cook at 180°C for 15 minutes, until crispy. Alternatively, preheat the oven to 200°C/180°C fan/400°F/Gas mark 6 and cook on a lined baking tray for 30 minutes until the chicken is cooked all the way through. Check they are cooked fully before serving.

Note These strips can be cooked straight from frozen! The strips can be frozen for up to 1 month.

chicken and broccoli alfredo

I never used to like broccoli, but as I have become older, I love how versatile it is and how great it tastes in so many different dishes, especially with pasta. I adore an alfredo, and one that is so easy to prepare for a weeknight dinner is even better. This dish can be put straight into the oven and cooked in the same tray that you froze it in.

MAKES 4 PORTIONS

150g (5½oz) dried pasta of
   your choice
1 garlic clove, finely
   chopped
50g (1¾oz) mushrooms, thinly
   sliced
1 small red onion, finely
   diced
100g (3½oz) spinach leaves
1 head of broccoli, cut into
   small florets
120g (4¼oz) low-fat cream
   cheese
3 skinless, boneless chicken
   breasts, diced
Low-calorie cooking spray
Sea salt and freshly ground
   black pepper

Prep time 10 minutes | **Cook time** 30 minutes | **Calorie count** 478 calories per portion

Par-cook the pasta in a saucepan of salted boiling water for 5 minutes, or until softened but not cooked (just before it is al dente).

Spray a frying pan (skillet) with some low-calorie cooking spray and place over a medium heat. Add the garlic, mushrooms and onion, season with a pinch of sea salt and black pepper and cook for 3 minutes until softened, then add the spinach and broccoli and fry for 3 minutes. Add the cream cheese and stir until the cheese has melted. Allow to cool.

Add the chicken to the cooled sauce and mix well, then transfer to the tray you are freezing it in (or a freezerproof oven dish). Cover with cling film (plastic wrap) and freeze.

The day before cooking, remove the tray from the freezer and allow the contents to thaw in the refrigerator for 24 hours.

When ready to cook, preheat the oven to 200°C/180°C fan/ 400°F/Gas mark 6, cook in the tray that you froze it in for 25 minutes.

Notes For this recipe, I like to use a disposable foil tray to freeze and cook the dish in.

Once frozen, the dish will keep for up to 3 months.

enchilada casserole

One of my earliest recipes that really took off on the blog was for 'I can't believe it's not enchiladas', as it was made with pasta instead of tortilla wraps. This dish is essentially like an enchilada lasagne. The filling can be frozen raw, then defrosted and layered into a casserole dish when ready to cook.

MAKES 4 PORTIONS

4 skinless, boneless chicken breasts, diced
1 large red (bell) pepper, deseeded and sliced into strips
1 yellow (bell) pepper, deseeded and sliced into strips
1 red onion, sliced
2 teaspoons ground cumin
2 teaspoons garlic granules
1 teaspoon smoked paprika
2 x 500g (1lb 2oz) cartons of passata (sieved tomatoes)
2 garlic cloves, minced
1 red chilli, deseeded and finely chopped (adjust according to your spice tolerance)
Sea salt and freshly ground black pepper

To assemble

4 tortilla wraps
160g (5½oz) reduced-fat Cheddar cheese, grated
Low-calorie cooking spray

Prep time 5 minutes | **Cook time** 30 minutes | **Calorie count** 520 calories per portion

Put the chicken, peppers, red onion, cumin, garlic granules, smoked paprika, passata, garlic and chilli in a large, heavy-duty freezer bag and season with a pinch each of salt and pepper. Remove as much air as possible, tightly seal and freeze.

The day before cooking, remove the bag from the freezer and allow the contents to thaw in the refrigerator for 24 hours.

Preheat the oven to 200°C/180°C fan/400°F/Gas mark 6. Spray an ovenproof dish with low-calorie cooking spray, then add two tortillas, letting them overlap. Add half the mixture on top, then add another layer of tortillas and top with the rest of the mixture. Top with the grated cheese, then bake in the oven for 30 minutes.

Notes The filling (minus the wraps and cheese) can be frozen ready to be assembled when you're ready to cook.

Once frozen, the filling will keep for up to 3 months.

garlic chicken and prosciutto pasta

This is an absolute favourite of mine from the blog, and every time I post it online people go crazy for it. It is also great for freezing as well. The garlicky chicken is packed full of flavour, with tasty prosciutto ham throughout.

MAKES 4 PORTIONS

1 onion, finely diced

1 red (bell) pepper, deseeded and thinly sliced

500g (1lb 2oz) skinless, boneless chicken breast, diced

1 teaspoon dried Italian herb mix

2 garlic cloves, minced

400g (14oz) dried pasta

1 x 500g (1lb 2oz) carton of passata (sieved tomatoes)

3 slices of prosciutto ham, cut into thin strips

160g (5½oz) extra-light Cheddar cheese, grated

Low-calorie cooking spray

Sea salt and freshly ground black pepper

Prep time 10 minutes | **Cook time** 32 minutes | **Calorie count** 480 calories per portion

Spray a frying pan (skillet) with some low-calorie cooking spray and place over a medium heat. Add the onion and sliced pepper and fry for 5 minutes until softened, then remove and set aside.

Put the pan back over a medium heat, spray with low-calorie cooking spray, add the diced chicken, sprinkle it with the Italian herbs and garlic and fry for 7 minutes until the chicken is cooked through.

Meanwhile, par-cook the pasta in a saucepan of salted boiling water for 5–6 minutes.

Add the passata and a pinch each of salt and pepper to the chicken in the pan and turn off the heat, then add the slices of prosciutto.

Drain the par-cooked pasta and pour it into a large ovenproof and freezerproof dish (or foil tray). Top with the passata and chicken and stir until everything is well mixed. Sprinkle with the grated cheese, cover with cling film (plastic wrap) and freeze.

The day before cooking, remove the dish or tray from the freezer and allow the contents to thaw in the refrigerator for 24 hours.

When ready to cook, preheat the oven to 200°C/180°C fan/ 400°F/Gas mark 6. Cook for 20 minutes, or until the dish is cooked through and the cheese is bubbling.

~~~~~

Notes For this recipe, I like to use a disposable foil tray to freeze and cook the dish in.

Once frozen, the dish will keep for up to 3 months.

chicken parmigiana casserole

Chicken parmigiana is an Italian-American dish based on the traditional Italian aubergine parmigiana – and this one is my own little twist on it. It is originally a crispy breaded chicken breast with a rich tomato sauce and melted mozzarella, but this twist combines all the elements with a breadcrumb topping. Perfect for freezing and cooking during the week!

MAKES 4 PORTIONS

500g (1lb 2oz) skinless, boneless chicken breast, diced

2 teaspoons dried basil

2 teaspoons minced garlic

1 teaspoon garlic granules

1 x 500g (1lb 2oz) carton of passata (sieved tomatoes)

240g (8½oz) wholemeal bread slices

2 tablespoons grated Parmesan

1 beef tomato, sliced

180g (6oz) ball of mozzarella

Low-calorie cooking spray

Sea salt and freshly ground black pepper

Prep time 10 minutes | **Cook time** 20 minutes | **Calorie count** 350 calories per portion

Put the chicken in a casserole dish or foil tray. Add the basil, garlic and garlic granules to the passata and season with a pinch each of salt and pepper, then pour the passata over the chicken.

Blitz the bread in a food processor to make breadcrumbs. Top the chicken and tomato with the breadcrumbs and sprinkle over the Parmesan, then add a layer of sliced tomato and torn mozzarella.

Allow to cool, then wrap in cling film (plastic wrap) and freeze.

The day before cooking, remove the tray or dish from the freezer and allow the contents to thaw in the refrigerator for 24 hours.

When ready to cook, preheat the oven to 200°C/180°C fan/400°F/Gas mark 6. Bake for 20 minutes or until the breadcrumbs have browned, the chicken is cooked through and the cheese has melted.

Notes For this recipe, I like to use a disposable foil tray to freeze and cook the dish in.

Once frozen, the casserole will keep for up to 3 months.

spinach and artichoke chicken

If you love a spinach and artichoke dip, then this dish is the one for you. It is inspired by the delicious dip with its amazing flavours, but made with succulent chicken breast. This 'dump and go' dinner is one you can prepare quickly, then put straight into the oven with very little prep. It is delicious served with rice.

MAKES 4 PORTIONS

4 skinless, boneless chicken breasts, diced

1 x 400g (14oz) tin of artichoke hearts, drained

100g (3½oz) baby spinach leaves

200ml (7fl oz/scant 1 cup) cool chicken stock

120g (4¼oz) low-fat cream cheese

40g (1½oz) grated Parmesan

2 garlic cloves, finely diced

Sea salt and freshly ground black pepper

Prep time 5 minutes | **Cook time** variable – see method | **Calorie count** 380 calories per portion

Put the diced chicken, drained artichoke hearts and spinach in a large, heavy-duty freezer bag.

Mix together the stock, cream cheese, Parmesan and garlic, and season with salt and pepper. Pour this over the ingredients in the freezer bag, remove as much air as possible, tightly seal and freeze.

The day before cooking, remove the bag from the freezer and allow the contents to thaw in the refrigerator for 24 hours.

When ready to cook, preheat the oven to 200°C/180°C fan/ 400°F/Gas mark 6. Transfer the thawed ingredients to a roasting tin and bake for 30 minutes, stirring halfway through, until the chicken is cooked.

Note Once frozen, the chicken will keep for up to 3 months.

sage and onion pork meatballs

I love these pork meatballs, and having them ready-made in the freezer makes them even better! If you like sage and onion stuffing, then this dish is the one for you. The meatballs and tomato sauce are perfect for slow cooking once defrosted as well. They are delicious served with pasta or mashed or boiled potatoes.

MAKES 3 PORTIONS

500g (1lb 2oz) extra-lean
   5%-fat minced (ground)
   pork
1 small onion, grated
1 teaspoon dried sage
2 garlic cloves, diced
1 x 500g (1lb 2oz) carton of
   passata (sieved tomatoes)
1 small onion, diced
1 teaspoon smoked paprika
Low-calorie cooking spray
Sea salt and freshly ground
   black pepper

Prep time 10 minutes | **Cook time** variable – see method | **Calorie count** 287 calories per portion

Preheat the oven to 200°C/180°C fan/400°F/Gas mark 6 and line a baking tray (sheet) with baking parchment.

Mix the minced pork, grated onion, sage and half of the garlic in a bowl with a little salt and pepper, then use your hands to roll the mixture into 12 equal-sized meatballs. Spray the lined tray with low-calorie cooking spray, lay the meatballs out on the lined baking tray and bake in the oven for 15 minutes.

Meanwhile, put the passata, the rest of the garlic, diced onion and the smoked paprika in a large, heavy-duty freezer bag with a little salt and pepper.

Once the meatballs are cooked, allow to cool, then add them to the freezer bag of passata. Remove as much air as possible, tightly seal and freeze.

The day before cooking, remove the bag from the freezer and allow the contents to thaw in the refrigerator for 24 hours.

Cook in the slow cooker on High for 4 hours, or bake in the oven in a casserole dish at 200°C/180°C fan/400°F/Gas mark 6 until cooked through and bubbling.

Note Once frozen, the meatballs and sauce will keep for up to 3 months.

rich pork ragu

This rich tomato-based pork ragu is so versatile and can be used in many ways once cooked. It requires very little preparation and can be put straight into a casserole dish to cook in the oven once thawed (or stored in a bag). It goes perfectly with pasta or rice.

MAKES 4 PORTIONS

1 large onion, finely diced

500g (1lb 2oz) extra-lean 5%-fat minced (ground) pork

1 large carrot, grated

250g (9oz) button mushrooms, finely chopped

1 red (bell) pepper, deseeded and finely diced

1 tablespoon tomato purée (paste)

2 x 400g (14oz) tins of chopped tomatoes

2 garlic cloves, finely chopped

1 teaspoon dried basil

1 teaspoon smoked paprika

1 tablespoon balsamic vinegar

3 teaspoons Worcestershire sauce

2 beef stock cubes, crumbled

Low-calorie cooking spray

Prep time 10 minutes | **Cook time** 30 minutes | **Calorie count** 480 calories per portion

Spray a frying pan (skillet) with some low-calorie cooking spray and place over a medium heat. Add the onion and fry for 3 minutes, then add the pork and fry for 5 minutes, breaking up the mince with a wooden spoon, until browned. Remove from the heat and allow to cool.

Put all the remaining ingredients in a large, heavy-duty freezer bag along with the cooled pork mixture, remove as much air as possible, tightly seal and freeze.

The day before cooking, remove the bag from the freezer and allow the contents to thaw in the refrigerator for 24 hours.

When ready to cook, preheat the oven to 200°C/180°C fan/ 400°F/Gas mark 6 and cook in a casserole dish for 30 minutes until fully cooked.

Note Once frozen, the ragu will keep for up to 3 months.

SLIMMING SNACKS

No matter how delicious our meals are, sometimes we just need a little something to help keep us going until the main meal.

People may often tell you that snacking between meals is a no-no, but if you enjoy some calorie-balanced snacks as part of a healthy meal plan, there is no reason why they can't be included too: there are many tasty treats that you can enjoy that won't break the calorie bank.

If you are following a lot of the recipes from this book, then you should have some spare calories left over to enjoy these sensational snacks.

Lots of these snacks can be prepared ahead of time and grabbed to eat when you're on the go, or prepared in just a few minutes.

There are both sweet and savoury snacks, which are perfect for taking to work in a packed lunch to help keep you going throughout the day.

Some of these have even been tested out by some of the Exeter City F.C. first team players, as I was writing and testing out recipes while preparing meals for them, and some of them had asked for some snacks.

My followers have been requesting more snack recipes, so it seems only right to include a whole chapter dedicated to some of my favourites.

baked feta and sesame bites

A delicious mix of sweet and savoury, these are a proper little speedy and tasty snack. The sesame seeds provide a crunchy coating, and the honey provides the sweetness to balance out the salty feta.

MAKES 2 PORTIONS

120g (4¼oz) reduced-fat feta cheese, cut into small chunks

½ teaspoon smoked paprika

3 tablespoons white sesame seeds

2 tablespoons runny honey

Prep time 5 minutes | **Cook time** 10 minutes | **Calorie count** 270 calories per portion

Preheat the oven to 200°C/180°C fan/400°F/Gas mark 6.

Sprinkle the feta with the paprika, then press it into the sesame seeds. As the feta is quite moist, I press it directly down into the sesame seeds so they stick. Make sure some are pressed into each side of the feta chunks.

Lay the feta chunks out on a baking tray (sheet), drizzle with the honey and bake in the oven for 10 minutes until golden.

Note These bites can also be air fried at 180°C for 6 minutes.

garlic bagel bites

These crunchy little bagel bites are packed with flavour and are a great substitute for crisps, and are amazing on their own or with a dip. You can leave the Parmesan out to save on some calories, or use a 'thin' bagel.

MAKES 2 PORTIONS

2 bagels
1 teaspoon garlic granules
1 teaspoon dried parsley
1 teaspoon smoked paprika
1 teaspoon grated Parmesan
Low-calorie cooking spray
Sea salt and freshly ground
    black pepper

Prep time 5 minutes | **Cook time** 10 minutes | **Calorie count** 255 calories per portion

Preheat the oven to 180°C/160°C fan/350°F/Gas mark 4.

Slice the bagels in half, not in the traditional way, but through the centre and the hole in the middle. Then cut them into round circles about 2.5mm thick. Put the slices in a bowl and spray generously with low-calorie cooking spray.

Add the garlic granules, parsley, paprika and Parmesan and season generously with salt and pepper. Mix well until all the slices are coated.

Spread the slices out on a baking tray (sheet), spray with low-calorie cooking spray and bake in the oven for 10 minutes, until golden and crispy.

Note The thinner you slice the bites, the more you get!

These bites can also be air fried at 180°C for 8 minutes.

crunchy chickpeas three ways

Roasted chickpeas are a new discovery for me, and have become a firm favourite snack. You can make them ahead of time and enjoy them all week, and I have included three of my favourite flavour combinations here.

MAKES 4 PORTIONS

2 x 400g (14oz) tins of
  chickpeas (garbanzo
  beans), drained and
  rinsed
1 tablespoon olive oil

Seasonings
BBQ

1 teaspoon smoked paprika
1 teaspoon onion powder
½ teaspoon garlic granules
¼ teaspoon chilli powder
Pinch each of sea salt and
  freshly ground black
  pepper

Garlic and rosemary

1 teaspoon garlic granules
1 teaspoon dried rosemary
Pinch each of sea salt and
  freshly ground black
  pepper

Lime and chilli

½ teaspoon chilli powder
  (adjust to your desired
  spice tolerance)
Grated zest and juice of
  1 lime
Pinch each of sea salt and
  freshly ground black
  pepper

Prep time 5 minutes | **Cook time** 35 minutes |
Calorie count 160 calories per portion

Preheat the oven to 200°C/180°C fan/400°F/Gas mark 6 and line a baking tray (sheet) with baking parchment.

Pat the chickpeas dry with paper towels: the more moisture you can remove, the crispier the chickpeas will be. Transfer to a bowl.

To make the BBQ seasoning, mix all the ingredients together and sprinkle over as a dry mix.

To make the Garlic and Rosemary seasoning, mix all the ingredients together and sprinkle over as a dry mix.

To make the Lime and Chilli seasoning, sprinkle the chilli over the chickpeas, then squeeze over the lime juice and sprinkle over the zest.

Add the olive oil to the chickpeas along with your choice of seasoning and mix well so that they are all evenly coated.

Lay them out on the lined baking tray and roast for 35 minutes, shaking them every now and again. The chickpeas will be golden and crunchy when ready, but keep an eye on them when they are cooking as they can turn perfect really quickly.

~~~~

Notes These will keep in an airtight container for up to 3 days.

These chickpeas can also be air fried at 180°C for 15 minutes, giving them a shake halfway through.

microwave crisps

I love the rustic crisps (chips) you get, but not only are they expensive, they're full of oil too. These crisps are so easy to make just in the microwave, and taste SO good! They are amazing with some sea salt.

MAKES 2 PORTIONS

2 potatoes, peeled

Iced water

2 teaspoons sea salt

Low-calorie cooking spray

Freshly ground black pepper

Prep time 10 minutes | **Cook time** 4 minutes | **Calorie count** 160 calories per portion

Slice the potatoes as thinly as possible – the thinner the better. A vegetable slicer (mandoline) works well. Place the slices in iced water for 3 minutes (this helps remove the starch and create crispy crisps).

Remove the slices from the water and place them on paper towels, making sure they're all dry.

Line a microwaveable plate with baking parchment, then add the potato slices, making sure there is no overlap.

Spray with low-calorie cooking spray and microwave on high for 2 minutes on one side, then flip the slices over and microwave for 2 minutes on the other side or until golden brown. All microwaves are different, so keep an eye to make sure they're not overdone.

They will crisp up even more as they cool down!

Sprinkle them with the sea salt and some pepper, or any seasoning of your choice and serve.

Note The crisps will keep in an airtight container for up to 2 days.

spinach and cheese filo bites

These little cheesy parcels are a great grab-and-go snack and are just as lovely hot or cold. Once you perfect them, they can be filled with a variety of different ingredients, such as chicken or ham.

MAKES ABOUT 6 PARCELS/BITES

270g (9½oz) filo (phyllo) pastry sheets (7 sheets)
Low-calorie cooking spray

For the filling

100g (3½oz) low-fat cream cheese
50g (1¾oz) baby spinach leaves
½ teaspoon dried oregano
¼ teaspoon garlic granules
½ teaspoon onion powder
Pinch each of sea salt and freshly ground black pepper

Prep time 5 minutes | **Cook time** 10 minutes | **Calorie count** 128 calories per parcel/bite

Preheat the oven to 180°C/160°C fan/350°F/Gas mark 4 and line a baking sheet with baking parchment.

Mix together all the filling ingredients in a bowl.

Pile the filo sheets on top of each other, then cut the stack into six 7.5cm (3 inch) squares.

Add half a tablespoon of mixture into the centre of each square. Gather up the corners and scrunch them at the top to cover the mixture inside. This doesn't have to look pretty, just needs to cover the filling.

Place the parcels on the lined baking sheet, spray with some low-calorie cooking spray and bake for 10 minutes until the filo is golden and crispy.

air-fried pickles with ranch dip

Fried pickles, or 'frickles', have to be one of my favourite things on the planet. Of course, the regular fried version isn't all that healthy...Which is why I created this air-fried version so that I can enjoy them without the guilt.

MAKES 2 PORTIONS

3 large pickled gherkins
   (dill pickles), cut into
   1cm (½ inch)-thick slices
Low-calorie cooking spray

For the coating
60g (2¼oz/generous ⅓ cup)
   plain (all-purpose) flour
½ tablespoon garlic granules
1 teaspoon smoked paprika
½ teaspoon onion powder
½ teaspoon chilli powder

For the ranch dip
2 tablespoons extra-light
   mayonnaise
1 tablespoon fat-free
   fromage frais
½ teaspoon dried parsley
½ teaspoon dried chives
¼ teaspoon onion powder
½ teaspoon garlic granules
¼ teaspoon each of sea salt
   and freshly ground black
   pepper
1 tablespoon pickle juice

Prep time 10 minutes | **Cook time** 6 minutes |
Calorie count 190 calories per portion

Pat the pickle slices dry with paper towels to remove any excess pickle juice.

Mix the coating ingredients in a bowl. Add the pickle slices and stir until coated. Add to the air-fryer tray and space them all evenly apart. Spray with some low-calorie cooking spray.

Set the air fryer to 180°C, then add the pickles and air fry for 3 minutes. Turn all the pickle slices over then fry for another 3 minutes.

Combine the ranch dip ingredients in a bowl.

Remove the pickles from the air fryer and serve with the dip.

Note These can also be baked in the oven on a lined baking tray (sheet) at 200°C/180°C fan/400°F/Gas mark 6 for 10 minutes.

mini mediterranean vegetable tarts

These tasty little vegetable tarts are perfect for lunchbox snacks. Feel free to use different vegetables according to what's in season or what you have to hand. You could even make these into a light lunch by serving with salad or cooked grains.

MAKES 6 TARTS

1 red (bell) pepper, deseeded and cut into small chunks

1 yellow (bell) pepper, deseeded and cut into small chunks

1 small red onion, cut into small chunks

1 small courgette (zucchini), trimmed and cut into small chunks

60g (2¼oz) cherry tomatoes, quartered

4 filo (phyllo) pastry sheets

Low-calorie cooking spray

Sea salt and freshly ground black pepper

Prep time 5 minutes | **Cook time** 30 minutes | **Calorie count** 105 calories per tart

Preheat the oven to 200°C/180°C fan/400°F/Gas mark 4 and spray 6 holes of a muffin tin with low-calorie cooking spray.

Place all the vegetables on a baking tray (sheet), spray with low-calorie cooking spray and season with salt and pepper, and roast for 20 minutes.

Cut each sheet of filo into six squares. Push each square into a muffin tin hole to form a tart case and repeat until you have 6 pastry cases composed of a 4-layer filo pastry shell. Spoon the roasted vegetables into the cases and bake for 10 minutes, until crisp and golden.

Remove from the oven and allow to cool.

~~~

Notes These tarts can also be air-fried at 180°C for 15 minutes. Air-fry the vegetables in the air-fryer tray first, for 5 minutes then air-fry the assembled tarts.

The tarts will keep in the refrigerator for up to 5 days.

jamaican-inspired beef patty wraps

Traditional Jamaican beef patties consist of a semi-circle of flaky pastry stuffed with a spicy meat filling. This quick, lower-calorie version is made with a tortilla wrap – they are easy to make, super delicious and perfect for air-fryer cooking as they come out extra crispy.

MAKES 4 PATTIES

½ onion, finely diced

1 red (bell) pepper, deseeded and finely diced

1 garlic clove, finely diced

250g (9oz) extra-lean 5%-fat minced (ground) beef

1 red chilli, deseeded and diced (adjust to taste)

1 teaspoon garam masala

1 teaspoon smoked paprika

1 teaspoon ground turmeric

Pinch of sea salt

½ teaspoon dried thyme

1 beef stock cube

1 tablespoon brown sauce

½ tablespoon Worcestershire sauce

4 mini tortilla wraps

1 egg, beaten, to glaze the patties

Low-calorie cooking spray

Prep time 10 minutes | **Cook time** 6 minutes | **Calorie count** 250 calories each, if making 2 from a wrap

Spray a large frying pan (skillet) with some low-calorie cooking spray and place over a medium heat. Add the onion, pepper and garlic and cook for 2 minutes until softened, then add the beef and cook for about 4 minutes, breaking up the mince with a wooden spoon, until browned.

Add the red chilli, garam masala, smoked paprika, turmeric, salt and thyme. Mix well and reduce the heat. Crumble in the stock cube, then add the brown sauce, Worcestershire sauce and a few tablespoons of water. Cook for about 5 minutes until a sauce forms – you may need to add a little more water if the mixture looks too dry. Remove from the heat and allow the patty mixture to cool slightly.

Put 2 tablespoons of the mixture into the centre of each of the mini wraps, then fold over and use an empanada press to crimp the edges, or just fold the edges over with your hands and use a fork to crimp them. I crimp with the mould as well as pressing with a fork to make sure no filling leaks out when cooking. Brush each patty with plenty of the beaten egg (this helps give it a golden colour), add to the air-fryer basket and cook at 180°C for 6 minutes, until golden and crispy. Serve hot or cold.

Note If you don't have an air fryer, you can bake the wraps on a baking tray (sheet) in the oven at 200°C/180°C fan/400°F/Gas mark 6 for 15 minutes until golden.

oat and yogurt cups

These little cups are so easy to make and can be prepped ahead at the weekend and eaten during the week.

MAKES 4 PORTIONS

60g (2¼oz) low-fat butter spread

2 tablespoons honey

1 tablespoon Lotus biscuit spread

160g (5½oz/¾ cup) porridge oats

8 tbsp fat-free vanilla yoghurt

Low-calorie cooking spray

Selection of fruit, such as strawberries and blueberries, to serve

Prep time 5 minutes | **Cook time** 15 minutes | **Calorie count** 190 calories per portion

Preheat the oven to 200°C/180°C fan/400°F/Gas mark 6 and spray 4 holes of a muffin tin with low-calorie cooking spray.

Put the butter, honey and biscuit spread in a microwaveable bowl and melt in the microwave in 10-second bursts, stirring regularly.

Add the oats to the melted butter mixture and stir well.

Put a spoonful of the oat mixture in a greased muffin hole and press down to make a cup, making sure you press down in the centre to make room for the yoghurt. Repeat with the remaining mixture to make 4 cups. Bake in the oven for 15 minutes, or until golden brown.

Remove from the oven and allow to cool fully before removing them from the tin. Take out each cup, then fill with yoghurt and a fruit topping of your choice.

Note Can be stored in the refrigerator for up to 4 days.

peanut and oat energy balls

This recipe was tested out on a few of the Exeter City F.C. first-team players – they had been asking for something sweet, and this recipe was a big hit. There's no need to bake them, and they can be prepped ahead at the weekend as a time-saver treat. They are super filling too, being crammed with protein!

Prep time 5 minutes | **Calorie count** 165 calories per portion

**MAKES 8 BALLS
(2 PER PORTION)**

3 tablespoons peanut butter
   (crunch or smooth)
2 tablespoons runny honey
100g (3½oz) dark chocolate
   chips (or raisins)
160g (5½oz/¾ cup) porridge
   oats
2 tablespoons flax seeds

Put the peanut butter and honey in a microwaveable dish and melt in the microwave in 10-second bursts.

Add the rest of the ingredients and mix well. If the mixture looks a little dry, you may need to add some more honey (and adjust the calories). The mixture should be wet enough that you can form the mixture into balls that will hold together.

Roll the mixture into 8 even-sized balls, then refrigerate.

Note These will keep in the refrigerator for up to 5 days.

QUICK

DESSERTS

When people just see my blog name, they often think I am a cake blog.

While I do enjoy baking, I have never claimed to be a 'star baker'. I think I can make really delicious cakes, but I've never been all that good at the decorating part. It's all about the taste though, isn't it?

If there was one thing that my followers have requested above all else, it would be some tasty low-calorie desserts. What could be better than desserts that are so simple, easy and delicious to prepare, as well as being calorie friendly too?

These desserts require very little effort and can be prepped really quickly. They also include some of my all-time favourites, but with a healthier twist.

A few of these have also been tested out on Exeter City players and staff on match days, with the cheesecake being a huge hit.

There are a couple of blog smash hits in here, as well as some new future favourites.

biscoff truffles

These are probably one of the tastiest treats I have ever made! I love a treat like this, and if consumed in moderation, these truffles are the perfect sweet morsel or dessert. Dip them into some fat-free Greek yoghurt, to coat, if you like (instead of the white chocolate). Try not to eat the whole batch in one go!

MAKES 23 TRUFFLE BALLS

100g (3½oz) Lotus biscuits,
   crushed into fine
   crumbs
3 tablespoons quark
Dash of vanilla extract
50g (1¾oz) white chocolate
1 teaspoon Lotus biscuit
   spread

Prep time 5 minutes, plus chilling time |
Calorie count 50 calories per truffle (this will vary depending on how many you make)

Mix most of the crushed biscuits (set aside a teaspoon of the crushed biscuits for finishing the truffles) and quark together in a bowl, with the vanilla extract, then roll the mixture into small balls – I made 23 out of this mix.

Break the white chocolate into pieces, place in a microwaveable bowl and microwave in 10-second intervals until melted, then stir in the Lotus biscuit spread. Dip the truffles in the melted white chocolate, then lay them out on a baking sheet.

Sprinkle the truffles with leftover biscuit crumbs and place in the refrigerator to set for 10 minutes.

vanilla mug cake

Is there anything better than a cake that you can prepare in just a few minutes in the microwave? This is the perfect speedy treat! All you need to do is add everything to a mug, microwave and serve with some fat-free yoghurt.

MAKES 1 CAKE

2 tablespoons plain (all-purpose) flour

1 tablespoon granulated sweetener

¼ teaspoon baking powder

2 tablespoons skimmed milk

1 teaspoon melted coconut oil

¼ teaspoon vanilla extract

To serve

3 tablespoons fat-free Greek vanilla yoghurt

Sprinkles (optional)

Prep time 5 minutes | **Cook time** 1 minute | **Calorie count** 220 calories per cake

Whisk together the flour, sweetener and baking powder in a microwaveable coffee mug (minimum 250ml/8fl oz capacity).

Whisk in the milk, melted coconut oil and vanilla extract until a cake batter forms. Microwave on high for about 1 minute, or until you see the cake rising.

Remove from the microwave, taking care as the mug will be hot. Check that the cake is moist and soft before serving it topped with yoghurt and optional sprinkles.

Note To make this vegan, substitute the milk for almond milk.

gooey chocolate brownies

These fudgy, gooey, tasty Nutella brownies are so quick to prepare – all you need to do is blend the ingredients in a food processor or blender and bake. These are a chocolate lovers' dream!

MAKES 12 BROWNIES

60g (2¼oz/½ cup) unsweetened cocoa powder

60g (2¼oz/generous 1 cup) granulated sweetener

90g (3¼oz/scant 1 cup) porridge oats

2 tablespoons fat-free Greek yoghurt

2 tablespoons skimmed milk

1 teaspoon baking powder

2 tablespoons Nutella

Prep time 5 minutes | **Cook time** 25 minutes | **Calorie count** 85 calories per brownie

Preheat the oven to 200°C/180°C fan/400°F/Gas mark 6 and line a baking tray (sheet) with baking parchment (I use a 35 x 24cm/14 x 9½in tray which makes 12 brownies).

Put the cocoa powder, sweetener, oats, yoghurt, skimmed milk and baking powder in a blender or food processor and blitz until smooth. If the mixture looks dry, add a little more yoghurt and blitz again. Pour half of the mixture into the lined baking tray, then melt the Nutella in a microwaveable bowl in the microwave in 10-second bursts and add it on top of the brownie mixture. Lightly mix before adding the remaining brownie mixture on top. Bake in the oven for 25 minutes until they have risen slightly and have a brownie-like top.

Remove from the oven and allow to cool, then cut into 12 squares.

Notes Bear in mind that the calorie count will change if you make more or fewer brownies.

The brownies can be refrigerated for up to 5 days.

protein chocolate chip cookie dough

The trend for eating cookie dough came over from America and it's essentially the dough before you bake a cookie. You can enjoy a whole portion of this without any of the guilt!

MAKES 2 PORTIONS

160g (5½oz/1½ cups) porridge oats

30g (1oz) vanilla protein powder (1 scoop)

½ teaspoon salt

75ml (2½fl oz/⅓ cup) oat milk

2 tablespoons maple syrup

2 tablespoons dark chocolate chips

Prep time 5 minutes, plus chilling time | **Calorie count** 380 calories per portion

Put the oats in a food processor and blitz until they form a fine powder, then transfer to a mixing bowl. Add the rest of the ingredients (except the dark chocolate chips) and mix until it forms a dough-like consistency. If it looks a little dry, add some more oat milk.

Mix in the chocolate chips, then transfer to a sealable container. Refrigerate for 10 minutes, then it is ready to serve.

Note I have made this recipe vegan, but the oat milk can be replaced with skimmed milk if you prefer.

chocolate caramel pudding

This recipe takes inspiration from an American pudding, and that doesn't just mean a dessert! It has a different consistency to a British sponge pudding, and is similar to what we call a mousse in the UK. Chocolate and caramel go so well together.

**MAKES 4 LARGE OR
6 SMALL PUDDINGS**

1 x 400ml (14fl oz) tin
    of low-fat coconut milk
1 tablespoon granulated
    sweetener
3 tablespoons maple syrup
½ teaspoon sea salt
125ml (4¼fl oz/generous
    ½ cup) skimmed milk
2 tablespoons cornflour
    (cornstarch)
1 teaspoon vanilla extract
2 teaspoons unsweetened
    cocoa powder

Prep time 2 minutes | **Cook time** 15 minutes |
Calorie count 220 calories per pudding (if making 4 large)

Whisk the coconut milk, granulated sweetener, maple syrup and salt in a saucepan. Bring to the boil over a medium-high heat, then reduce the heat and simmer for about 10 minutes, stirring, until the mixture thickens.

Mix together the milk, cornflour, vanilla extract and cocoa powder and add to the coconut milk mixture. Continue to whisk for 5 minutes until it thickens some more and is darker in colour.

Pour into 4 or 6 heatproof glasses to serve. It can be enjoyed straight away, while warm, or left in the refrigerator to cool down and firm up.

ginger and lemon cheesecakes

This zesty cheesecake is high in protein and extra filling. The zesty lemon and spicy ginger are a perfect partnership. The protein yoghurts are made using cream cheese, making them perfect for desserts like this.

MAKES 2 PORTIONS

2 x 200g (7oz) tubs of
   vanilla protein yoghurt
Juice of 1 lemon, plus
   grated lemon zest to
   finish

For the base

1 tablespoon low-fat spread
4 gingernut biscuits

Prep time 5 minutes | **Calorie count** 250 calories per portion

First, make the base. Melt the spread in a microwaveable dish in the microwave and crush the gingernut biscuits to fine crumbs. Combine the biscuit crumbs and spread, then press half of the mixture down to form a base in each ramekin.

Combine the yoghurt and lemon juice, then add this on top of the ginger biscuit base. Top with lemon zest to serve.

Note I like to make these in mini ramekins - I feel like every home has a stash of these left over from other desserts!

key lime pie

I love key lime pie, and this is my much healthier version. The real thing is made with key lime juice, egg yolks and sweetened condensed milk, but this adapted recipe is not only just as delicious but much easier to prepare too! If you can't find key limes, normal limes will do.

Prep time 5 minutes | **Calorie count** 320 calories per pie

MAKES 2 PIES

1 teaspoon granulated
   sweetener
200g (7oz/scant 1 cup)
   fat-free Greek yoghurt
2 limes, plus grated lime
   zest to finish

For the crumb

60g (2¼oz/scant ½ cup) plain
   (all-purpose) flour
2 tablespoons honey
2 tablespoons low-fat butter
   spread (or almond butter)

Combine the ingredients for the crumb in a microwaveable bowl – the mixture should have a dry dough consistency. Microwave for 1½ minutes, stirring at regular intervals, until it becomes more like a crumble.

Add the sweetener to the yoghurt, then squeeze in the juice from the limes. Mix well.

Add a layer of the crumb to the base of two glasses, then add the sweetened lime yoghurt and continue to layer up the crumb and lime yoghurt until used up. Top with lime zest to serve.

'toyah's tasty tiramisu

Tiramisu is my mum's speciality pudding, so I have loved it since I was a child. If you are trying to watch the calories, however, it is not that healthy! This is my guilt-free version. Don't be put off by the rice cakes – they really work, and it tastes so good!

Prep time 5 minutes | **Calorie count** 230 calories per portion

MAKES 2 PORTIONS

6 plain, unsalted rice cakes
100ml (3½fl oz/scant ½ cup)
    black coffee, left to
    cool
200g (7oz/scant 1 cup)
    low-fat cream cheese
    (or protein yoghurt)
6 tablespoons fat-free Greek
    yoghurt
1 teaspoon granulated
    sweetener
1 teaspoon vanilla extract
2 teaspoons unsweetened
    cocoa powder, for
    sprinkling

Put the rice cakes in a bowl and pour over the cooled black coffee. Leave to soak while you prepare the rest of the dish.

Mix together the cream cheese, Greek yoghurt and sweetener in a bowl.

Put 2 of the soaked rice cakes in a large ramekin or dish. Add a couple of tablespoons of the cream cheese mixture and spread it out evenly. Add another 2 rice cakes and layer some more of the cream cheese mixture, then repeat with another layer of rice cakes and cream cheese mixture. Sprinkle the cocoa powder over the top, then put in the refrigerator until ready to serve.

sticky toffee pudding

This combination of sticky toffee pudding flavours and baked oats makes one super tasty and easy dessert. It is a British classic and is perfect for an after-dinner treat. The dates give the dish its toffee sweetness and a moist texture.

MAKES 2 PORTIONS

60g (2¼oz) pitted dates, cut into small pieces
80g (2¾oz/¾ cup) porridge oats
½ teaspoon baking powder
½ teaspoon ground cinnamon
Pinch of salt
200ml (7fl oz/scant 1 cup) skimmed milk
Low-calorie cooking spray
Fat-free vanilla Greek yoghurt, to serve

Prep time 5 minutes | **Cook time** 10-15 minutes | **Calorie count** 320 calories per pudding

Preheat the oven to 200°C/180°C fan/400°F/Gas mark 6.

Grease a 13 x 9cm (5 x 3½ inch) baking dish with some low-calorie cooking spray.

Put the date pieces in a heatproof bowl, pour over 100ml (3½fl oz/scant ½ cup) boiled water and set aside to soak for 5 minutes until the dates have softened.

Blitz the oats in a food processor or blender until finely ground to a powder, then transfer to a mixing bowl. Add the baking powder, cinnamon and salt, then drain the soaked dates and add them in as well. Add the milk and mix to form a batter.

Pour the mixture into the greased baking dish and cook in the preheated oven for 15 minutes until golden. Serve with the yoghurt.

Note These can be cooked in an air-fryer, too: set the air fryer to 180°C and cook for 10-12 minutes.

salted caramel apple crumble

Apple crumble is one of my favourite desserts, and this super easy caramel sauce takes it to the next level! Caramel tastes even better with a little pinch of sea salt, there is something magical about the sweet and savoury pairing.

MAKES 4 PORTIONS

2 large cooking apples, peeled, cored and finely diced
1 teaspoon cinnamon
½ teaspoon ground nutmeg
1 teaspoon granulated sweetener

For the crumble

70g (2½oz/scant ½ cup) plain (all-purpose) flour
70g (2½oz/¾ cup) porridge oats
1 teaspoon ground cinnamon
1 tablespoon maple syrup
1 tablespoon coconut oil

For the salted caramel sauce

2 tablespoons coconut oil
2 tablespoons maple syrup
2 tablespoons smooth almond butter
Pinch of sea salt

Prep time 5 minutes | **Cook time** 20 minutes | **Calorie count** 330 calories per portion

Preheat the oven to 200°C/180°C fan/400°F/Gas mark 6.

Put the apples in a 16cm (6½ inch) square or similarly sized ovenproof dish. Sprinkle with the cinnamon, nutmeg and sweetener and mix to coat. Bake in the oven for 5 minutes.

Mix the dry crumble ingredients together in a bowl, then add the maple syrup, coconut oil and a few tablespoons of water – a little at a time – mixing until it forms a crumble consistency.

Make the caramel sauce by melting the coconut oil and maple syrup together in a microwaveable bowl in the microwave in 10-second bursts, then remove and whisk in the almond butter and sea salt for about 30 seconds until smooth.

Remove the apples from the oven and drizzle half the sauce over the top. Add the crumble topping and bake for 15 minutes until golden. Drizzle with the rest of the sauce and serve.

Note The crumble can be refrigerated for up to 5 days. Reheat fully before serving.

meal plans

We all have busy lives – for those who work full-time, lunch can be the most complicated meal of the day. You may not have access to a full kitchen at lunchtime, making it much harder to cook anything fresh. For others, finding time to prepare dinner can be a challenge, when all you want to do is relax and rest.

I've put together two meal plans to help you stick to your slimming journey, whatever your lifestyle.

The first meal plan is designed for those who are looking for delicious lunches that can be prepared at the weekend and then taken to work to be reheated. The breakfasts and dinners are freshly made, and because all of the recipes in this book are slimming and speedy, they still won't take too much time and effort to prepare.

The second plan caters for everyone who is looking for an easy evening routine. By utilising the slow cooker, these recipes allow you to simply 'set it and forget it', so that you can come home to a satisfying, flavourful, ready-to-eat meal after a long day – all with minimal effort. The lunches in this meal plan have been taken from the Batch-cook Sunday chapter, so a bit of time spent at the weekend can set you up for the week.

Both plans are based on 1500 calories per day (although, of course, feel free to adjust this to your needs), with calories left over on each day for side dishes and extras – the perfect opportunity to try some of the tasty snacks or delicious sweet treats in the book.

	BREAKFAST	LUNCH	DINNER	TOTAL CALORIES
MONDAY	Sticky Honey, Lime, Halloumi and Avocado Wrap (550 calories) see page 34	Curried Cauliflower Soup (150 calories) see page 128	Chicken Fajita Pasta (450 calories) see page 66	1150
TUESDAY	Banana Bread Pancakes (548 calories) see page 20	Smoky Bean Burrito Bowls (520 calories) see page 134	Soy, Garlic and Chilli Noodles (250 calories) see page 81	1318
WEDNESDAY	Sausage and Hash Brown One-pot Scramble (518 calories) see page 41	Creamy Cajun Bacon Tagliatelle (340 calories) see page 151	Smash Burgers (530 calories) see page 84	1388
THURSDAY	'Posh' Egg on Toast (420 calories) see page 33	Lasagne Soup (280 calories) see page 131	Thai Red Curry Noodle Bowl (455 calories) see page 93	1155
FRIDAY	Mixed Berry French Toast Cups (480 calories) see page 23	Spicy Lamb and Feta Filo Pie (450 calories) see page 154	Sticky Turkey Meatballs (400 calories) see page 69	1330
SATURDAY	Turkish Egg Toast (490 calories) see page 28	Italian-style Veggie and Halloumi Pesto Bake (320 calories) see page 140	Pepperoni Pizza Macaroni (460 calories) see page 52	1270
SUNDAY	Smoky Spinach Eggs (260 calories) see page 37	Spicy Sausage Casserole and Dumplings (550 calories) see page 152	Naan Bread Pizza (535 calories) see page 78	1390

	BREAKFAST	LUNCH	DINNER	TOTAL CALORIES
MONDAY	Chocolate and Caramel Cheesecake Overnight Oats (435 calories) see page 25	Sweet Chilli Chicken Noodles (523 calories) see page 141	Beef Curry (350 calories) see page 120	1308
TUESDAY	Sausage and Hash Brown One-pot Scramble (518 calories) see page 41	Spicy, Sticky Halloumi with Orzo and Chickpeas (490 calories) see page 136	Pulled Smoked Paprika Jackfruit (225 calories) see page 103	1233
WEDNESDAY	Vegan Breakfast Skillet (350 calories) see page 38	Mustardy Chicken and Bacon Hot Pot (470 calories) see page 144	Chilli Con Carne Rice (570 calories) see page 117	1390
THURSDAY	Smoky Spinach Eggs (260 calories) see page 37	White Turkey Chilli (490 calories) see page 147	Korean-style Beef Noodles (520 calories) see page 118	1270
FRIDAY	Mixed Berry French Toast Cups (480 calories) see page 23	Creamy Cajun Bacon Tagliatelle (340 calories) see page 151	Creamy Boursin, Chorizo and Chicken Casserole (440 calories) see page 112	1260
SATURDAY	Peanut Butter Brownie Overnight Oats (520 calories) see page 26	Honey, Lemon and Garlic Chicken Thighs (270 calories) see page 142	Hunter's Chicken Dinner (570 calories) see page 110	1360
SUNDAY	Banana Bread Pancakes (548 calories) see page 20	Lasagne Soup (280 calories) see page 131	Slow-cooker Roast Beef Dinner (580 calories) see page 125	1408

OVEN TEMP	OVEN TEMP (FAN)	AIR FRYER TEMP	OVEN MINS	AIR FRYER MINS
180ºC	160ºC	140ºC	10 mins	8 mins
190ºC	170ºC	150ºC	15 mins	12 mins
200ºC	180ºC	160ºC	20 mins	16 mins
210ºC	190ºC	170ºC	25 mins	20 mins
220ºC	200ºC	180ºC	30 mins	24 mins
230ºC	210ºC	190ºC	35 mins	28 mins
240ºC	220ºC	200ºC	40 mins	32 mins
			45 mins	36 mins
			50 mins	40 mins
			55 mins	44 mins
			1 hour	48 mins

Temperatures and cooking times are for guidance only. Cooking times may vary depending on the appliance used. Ensure that you check that all food is cooked thoroughly before serving. More air fryer recipes are available at latoyah.co.uk

index

about
the author

I'm Latoyah. I am the creator of the popular blog Sugar Pink Food, where I share my low-calorie, slimming-friendly recipes. I have spent my life living in beautiful Devon, in the south-west of England, and have lived in Devon's capital, Exeter, since I was 18.

I have always been passionate about creating delicious dishes with a healthy touch, feeding friends and family with tasty treats, and coming up with fabulous 'fakeaways'. I started my website as a place to store recipes as I could never seem to recreate the same dish twice, and it started to build a following via social media. The popularity of my website grew over the years, and has now received over 20 million views, creating a large and loyal social media following.

I was dubbed the 'Queen of the Fakeaway' by the national press after recreating low-calorie versions of the best-loved takeaway dishes at home, with my blog being featured in publications including the *Metro*, *Daily Mail*, *My London*, *Devon Live* and the *Daily Star*.

I released my first book, *Healthy Home Cooking*, in January 2020 and my second book, *Slimming and Tasty*, in 2022. In 2021 I appeared as a judge on Channel 4's *Beat the Chef*.

f @sugarpinkfood
○ @sugarpinkfood
Website: https://www.latoyah.co.uk/

acknowledgements

I would like to thank my friends, Emma, Craig, James, Connor and David, for being so supportive throughout this process, both for this book and the first.

To my parents, for always supporting me, and to Nanny Jean and Grandad Brian for being my biggest fans – I hope I'm still making you all proud!

To Claire, for being there and for pulling me out of self-doubt every time – and for putting up with the recipes being plastered on our wall for months!

To Nick, for the daily support when writing everything up and for keeping me on track.

To the football crew for making fun of me whenever I mentioned I was 'writing a book'... and to the current and former ECFC players for testing some of the recipes, especially Tim and Jamal.

To Emily and Lucy, who are amazing at putting this all together, as well as Uyen and Sam for the incredible images in this book.

To everyone over the years who chose to follow and support me on social media, this wouldn't be happening without your ongoing interest in what I create, so thank you for being here.

To you, reading this, thank you for taking the time to read this book (or perhaps you just skipped to the end!) – I hope you find a new favourite recipe.

First published in Great Britain in 2023 by Greenfinch
An imprint of Quercus Editions Ltd
Carmelite House
50 Victoria Embankment
London
EC4Y 0DZ

An Hachette UK company

A CIP catalogue record for this book is available from the British Library.

HB ISBN 978-1-52942-954-1

eBook ISBN 978-1-52942-955-8

10 9 8 7 6 5 4 3 2 1

Design by Sarah Pyke
Photography by Uyen Luu
Food styling by Sam Dixon
Prop styling and project editing by Lucy Kingett

Printed and bound in China

Papers used by Greenfinch are from well-managed forests
and other responsible sources.

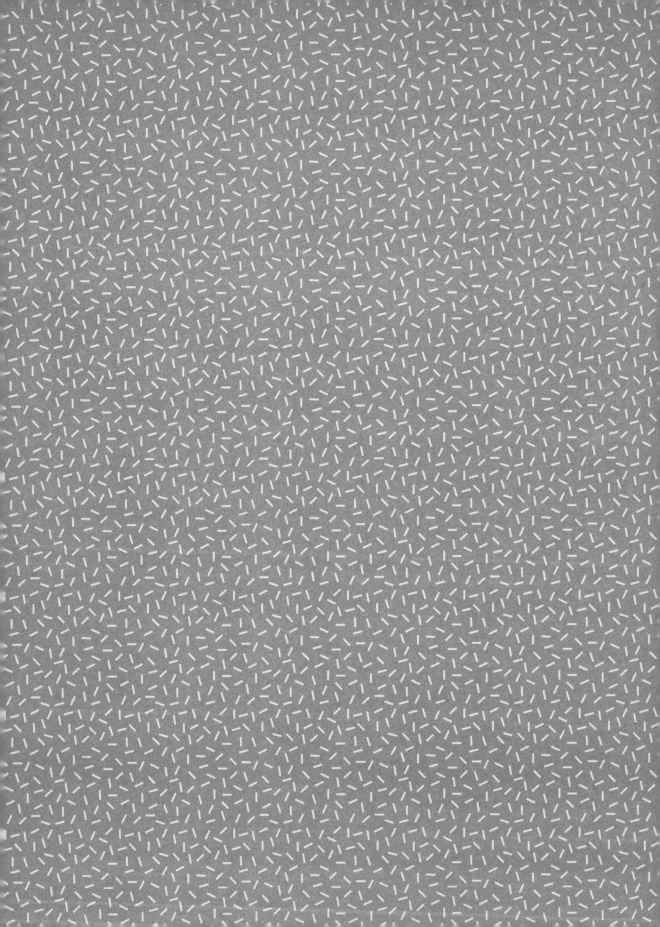